25 Days to
Better Thinking
&
Better Living

25 Days to Better Thinking & Better Living

A Guide for Improving Every Aspect of Your Life

Dr. Linda Elder and Dr. Richard Paul

An Imprint of Pearson Education
Upper Saddle River, NJ • New York • London • San Francisco • Toronto
Sydney • Tokyo • Singapore • Hong Kong • Cape Town • Madrid
Paris • Milan • Munich • Amsterdam

Vice President, Editor-in-Chief: Tim Moore
Executive Editor: Jim Boyd
Editorial Assistant: Susan Abraham
Development Editor: Russ Hall
Associate Editor-in-Chief and Director of Marketing: Amy Neidlinger
Cover Designer: Alan Clements
Managing Editor: Gina Kanouse
Senior Project Editor: Lori Lyons
Copy Editor: Gayle Johnson
Senior Indexer: Cheryl Lenser
Proofreader: Debbie Williams
Interior Designer/Senior Compositor: Gloria Schurick
Manufacturing Buyer: Dan Uhrig

© 2006 by Pearson Education, Inc.
Publishing as Prentice Hall
Upper Saddle River, New Jersey 07458

Prentice Hall offers excellent discounts on this book when ordered in quantity for bulk
purchases or special sales. For more information, please contact U.S. Corporate and Government
Sales, 1-800-382-3419, corpsales@pearsontechgroup.com. For sales outside the U.S., please
contact International Sales, 1-317-581-3793, international@pearsontechgroup.com.

Company and product names mentioned herein are the trademarks
or registered trademarks of their respective owners.

Printed in the United States of America

First Printing, March 2006

ISBN 0-13-173859-3

Pearson Education LTD.
Pearson Education Australia PTY, Limited.
Pearson Education Singapore, Pte. Ltd.
Pearson Education North Asia, Ltd.
Pearson Education Canada, Ltd.
Pearson Educatión de Mexico, S.A. de C.V.
Pearson Education—Japan
Pearson Education Malaysia, Pte. Ltd.

This product is printed digitally on demand.

Library of Congress Cataloging-in-Publication Data is on file.

To all those who use their thinking to expose hypocrisy and self-deception, and who work to create what is now but a remote dream—a just and humane world.

This page intentionally left blank

Contents

"The key to every man is his thought."
—Emerson

"Of all knowledge, the wise and good seek most to know themselves."
—Shakespeare

"Do you want to know the man against whom you have most reason to guard yourself? Your looking-glass will give you a very fair likeness of his face."
—Whately

"The first step to knowledge is to know that we are ignorant."
—Cecil

"The more you practice what you know, the more shall you know what to practice."
—W. Jenkin

"Thinking is the hardest work there is, which is the probable reason why so few engage in it."
—Henry Ford

Acknowledgments

A special acknowledgment is due to Gerald Nosich—dedicated thinker, exemplary scholar, lifelong friend, and colleague.

About the Authors

Dr. Linda Elder is an educational psychologist, Executive Director of the Center for Critical Thinking, and President of the Foundation for Critical Thinking. She is highly published and has done original research into the relation of thought and emotion and into the stages of critical thinking development. She is a regular keynoter at the International Conference on Critical Thinking, is highly sought after as a presenter, and is a recognized leader in critical thinking.

Dr. Richard Paul is Director of Research and Professional Development at the Center for Critical Thinking and Chair of the National Council for Excellence in Critical Thinking. He is an internationally recognized authority on critical thinking, with nine books and more than 200 articles on the subject. His views on critical thinking have been canvassed in the *New York Times, Education Week, The Chronicle of Higher Education, American Teacher, Reader's Digest, Educational Leadership, Newsweek,* and *U.S. News and World Report.*

The works of Linda Elder and Richard Paul have been translated into Spanish, French, German, Italian, Japanese, and Chinese. Translations are underway in Russian, Malay, and Korean. The growing demand for translations into increasing numbers of languages testifies to the emerging international recognition of the importance of critical thinking in human life and work and of the authoritative nature of the contribution of Paul and Elder in the field.

The Foundation for Critical Thinking seeks to promote essential change in society through the cultivation of fair-minded critical thinking, thinking predisposed toward intellectual empathy, humility, perseverance, integrity, and responsibility. In a world of accelerating change, intensifying complexity, and increasing interdependence, critical thinking is now a requirement for economic and social survival. Contact the Foundation for Critical Thinking at www.criticalthinking.org.

This page intentionally left blank

Preface

"Thinking leads man to knowledge. He may see and hear, and read and learn whatever he pleases, and as much as he pleases; he will never know anything of it, except that which he has thought over, that which by thinking he has made the property of his own mind."
—Pestalozzi

There is nothing we do as humans that does not involve thinking. Our thinking tells us what to believe, what to reject, what is important, what is unimportant, what is true, what is false, who are our friends, who are our enemies, how we should spend our time, what jobs we should pursue, where we should live, who we should marry, how we should parent. Everything we know, believe, want, fear, and hope for, our thinking tells us.

It follows, then, that the quality of our thinking is the primary determinant of the quality of our lives. It has implications for how we go about doing literally everything we do.

The quality of your work is determined by the quality of your thinking as you reason through the problems you face as you work. The quality of your relationships is determined by the thinking you do about and in those relationships. Right now, as you read this book, the very sense you make of it is a product of your thinking. Your ability to understand and internalize the ideas it contains will be determined by the quality of your thinking as you read it.

Therefore, learning to think at the highest level of quality, or to think critically, is too important to leave to chance. Critical thinking is the disciplined art of ensuring that you use the best thinking you are capable of in any set of circumstances. Through developed critical capacities, you can take command of the thinking that commands you.

No matter what your circumstance or goals, no matter where you are or what problems you face, you are better off if you are in control of your thinking. As a professional, parent, citizen, lover, friend, shopper—in every realm and situation of your life—skilled thinking pays off. Poor thinking, in contrast, inevitably causes problems, wastes time and energy, and engenders frustration and pain.

Becoming a critical thinker requires that you learn to observe, monitor, analyze, assess, and reconstruct thinking of many sorts in many dimensions of human life. It requires building important habits of mind. It has implications for every act that takes place in your mind. It requires a special form of dedication and perseverance, honesty and integrity. It can be done only if taken seriously and pursued throughout a lifetime.

This book shows you how to use your mind to improve your mind. Each of the ideas in this book can help you take command of the mind that is controlling your thoughts, emotions, desires, and behavior.

Our hope is not in a miracle transformation, but in laying a foundation for your future intellectual and emotional growth. We are merely scratching the surface of deep and complex topics. We do not provide a quick fix, but rather places to begin. When you begin to take your intellectual growth seriously, you begin to see payoffs in every part of your life.

But first, you must wake up your mind. You must begin to understand your mind. You must begin to see when it is causing you problems. You must begin to see when it is causing others problems. You must learn how to trap it when it tries to hide from itself (using one of the many forms of self-deception at which it is naturally skilled). You must discover some of the trash and nonsense you have unknowingly taken in during years of passive absorption—to which all of us are subject. This book shows you how to begin.

The quality of your life is determined by the quality of your thinking.

Thinking gets us into trouble because we often

- are unclear, muddled, or confused
- jump to conclusions
- fail to think-through implications
- lose track of our goals
- are unrealistic
- focus on the trivial
- do not notice contradictions
- accept inaccurate information
- ask vague questions
- give vague answers
- ask loaded questions
- ask irrelevant questions
- confuse questions of different types
- answer questions we are not competent to answer
- come to conclusions based on inaccurate or irrelevant information
- ignore information that does not support our view
- make inferences not justified by our experience
- distort data and state it inaccurately
- fail to notice the inferences we make
- come to unreasonable conclusions
- fail to notice our assumptions
- often make unjustified assumptions
- miss key ideas
- use irrelevant ideas
- form confused ideas
- form superficial concepts
- misuse words
- ignore relevant viewpoints
- cannot see issues from points of view other than our own
- confuse issues of different types
- are unaware of our prejudices
- think narrowly
- think imprecisely
- think illogically
- think one-sidedly
- think simplistically
- think hypocritically
- think superficially
- think ethnocentrically
- think egocentrically
- think irrationally
- fail to reason well through problems
- make poor decisions
- are poor communicators
- have little insight into our ignorance

Improve Your Thinking, Improve Your Life

This book is about how to improve your thinking to improve your life. Why thinking? Why is thinking significant? Why try to improve your thinking?

The answer is simple: only through thinking can you change whatever it is about your life that needs changing (even the parts you don't know need changing). Only through thinking can you take command of your future. Sound too simple? Read on.

Humans constantly think. Indeed, thinking is the main thing we do. From the minute we wake up in the morning, we begin thinking. During all of our waking hours, we are thinking. We cannot escape our thinking, even if we want to. Right now you are thinking about whether to take seriously what we are saying. In other words, thinking is happening in your mind every moment of your waking life, structuring your feelings, shaping your desires, and guiding your actions.[1] The way you think about parenting determines how you parent. The way you think about your financial situation determines the financial decisions you make. The way you think when you are at work determines how you function on the job.

The problem is that human thinking is often flawed. Many of our regrettable actions emerge from faulty reasoning. In fact, problems in thinking lead to more problems in life than perhaps any other single variable. They lead to conflict and war, pain and frustration, cruelty and suffering.

Yet, most people are content with their thinking. Because the development of thinking typically is not valued in human societies, people don't tend to trace the problems in their lives to problems in their thinking. Instead, they often live the whole of their lives without recognizing the leading role that thinking plays in it.

To improve your quality of life significantly, you must begin to take thinking seriously—to become a student, if you will, of thinking. You must begin to observe thinking, examine it, witness its power in action. You must begin to discipline your thinking through knowledge of thinking, and you should practice using that knowledge (of thinking) daily. You must begin to

---

[1] For an introduction to the relationships between thinking, feeling, and wanting, see The Thinker's Guide to the Human Mind, by Elder, L. and R. Paul, The Foundation for Critical Thinking (2002), www.criticalthinking.org.

analyze your thinking, assess your thinking, improve your thinking. You must engage in *critical* thinking.

This book explores some of the basic facts about thinking. Although the study of thinking and its relationship to emotions and desires are complex, its foundations are quite simple. The trick is to use basic principles systematically to change your life for the better. In other words, the trick is to put critical thinking into action in your life. You can learn it. You can use it. This book provides some of the building blocks.

Could Your Thinking Be Your Problem?

To begin to take thinking seriously, you must first recognize the inherently flawed nature of human thought in its "normal" state. Put another way, without active intervention, human thinking naturally develops problems. For example, humans are prejudiced. We stereotype one another. We are often hypocritical. We sometimes justify in our own minds policies and practices that result in stealing, killing, and torture. We often ignore important problems that we could, with determination and good thinking, solve—problems such as world hunger, poverty, and homelessness.

What is more, when we behave irrationally, our behavior usually seems reasonable to us. When challenged, the mind says (to itself), "Why are these people giving me a hard time? I'm just doing what makes sense. Any reasonable person would see that!" In short, we naturally think that our thinking is fully justified. As far as we can tell, we are only doing what is right and proper and reasonable. Any fleeting thoughts suggesting that we might be at fault typically are overcome by more powerful self-justifying thoughts: "I don't mean any harm. I'm just! I'm fair! It's the others who are wrong!"

It is important to recognize this self-justifying nature of the human mind as its *natural state*. In other words, humans don't have to learn self-justifying, self-serving, self-deceptive thinking and behavior. These patterns are innate in every one of us. How does self-deception work in the mind? In other words, how can it be that we can see ourselves as right even when readily available evidence proves us wrong? One powerful reason is the mind's *native* ability to represent unreasonable thoughts as perfectly reasonable. Indeed, this is perhaps the most significant reason that humans fail to recognize their own irrationality.

For example, consider the female supervisor who, after interviewing both male and female applicants, always hires women[2]. This supervisor considers herself unbiased and objective. When asked why she hires only female employees, she most likely would give reasons to support her decisions—facts, for example, about the applicants' work experiences, skills, and so forth. In supporting her hiring decisions, she would see herself as even-handed, as simply trying to hire the best employees for the job. Indeed, the only way she can feel justified *in her own mind* is to see herself as behaving objectively. In other words, biased thinking appears to the mind as dispassionate, unprejudiced, impartial thinking. We don't see ourselves as wrong. Rather, we see ourselves as right, as doing what is most reasonable in the situation, even when we are dead wrong.

Consider the police officer who often uses excessive force during arrests. This officer likely sees himself as giving criminals what they deserve, getting them off the streets so they can't harm innocent people. He couldn't act in this way if he recognized the role that prejudice and the desire for power were playing in his thinking, if he could see that he was irrationally using unnecessary power and force over others who were unable to defend themselves. In his own mind he is professional and just. However cruel he may be, he doesn't see himself as such.

Welcome to human nature. We are all, to varying degrees, prejudiced. We all stereotype and deceive ourselves. We see ourselves as possessing *the truth*. Yet we all fall prey to human egocentricity—although not to the same degree. None of us will ever be a perfect thinker, but we can all be *better* thinkers.

To develop as a thinker, you need to work daily to bring what is unconscious in your thinking to the level of consciousness. You need to discover the problems that exist in your thinking and face them. Only then can you make significant improvements in your thinking and your life. Inherent in human nature is the capacity to rise above your native egocentric patterns of thought. You can use your mind to educate your mind. You can use your thinking to change your thinking. You can "remake" or "transform" yourself. It is this side of your nature that we hope to stimulate as you work through and internalize the ideas in this book.

---

[2] Consider also the male supervisor who hires only men.

A How-to List for Dysfunctional Living

One of the ways you can enhance the power of your mind is by learning to create contrasts and oppositions that make clear precisely what you need to avoid. In other words, by making poor habits of thought more and more explicit, you get better and better at avoiding them.

We will now illustrate this strategy by constructing a set of rules that no reasonable person would knowingly follow. By illuminating dysfunctional, even pathological, ways of thinking, it becomes obvious how easy it is to fall prey to them without recognizing yourself doing so.

Consider the following, and ask yourself how many of these dysfunctional ways of thinking you engage in:

1. **Surround yourself with people who think like you.** Then no one will criticize you.

2. **Don't question your relationships.** You then can avoid dealing with problems within them.

3. **If critiqued by a friend or lover, look sad and dejected** and say, "I thought you were my friend!" or "I thought you loved me!"

4. **When you do something unreasonable, always be ready with an excuse.** Then you won't have to take responsibility. If you can't think of an excuse, look sorry and say, "I can't help how I am!"

5. **Focus on the negative side of life.** Then you can make yourself miserable and blame it on others.

6. **Blame others for your mistakes.** Then you won't have to feel responsible for your mistakes. Nor will you have to do anything about them.

7. **Verbally attack those who criticize you.** Then you don't have to bother listening to what they say.

8. **Go along with the groups you are in.** Then you won't have to figure out anything for yourself.

9. **Act out when you don't get what you want.** If questioned, look indignant and say, "I'm just an emotional person. At least I don't keep my feelings bottled up!"

10. **Focus on getting what you want.** If questioned, say, "If I don't look out for number one, who will?"

As you can see, this list would be almost laughable if these irrational ways of thinking didn't lead to problems in life. But they do. And often. Only when you are faced with the absurdity of dysfunctional or even pathological thinking and can see it at work in your life do you have a chance to alter it. The strategies outlined in this book presuppose your willingness to do so.

Taking Your Thinking Seriously

Our goal is to help you begin to think *critically* about your thinking— to think about the ways in which your thinking might be causing problems for you or others. As you work through the ideas in this book, simple ideas intelligently applied, you will begin to improve the habits of your mind. You will become aware of your thinking. When you do, you will assess it. When you assess it, you will improve it.

Think of yourself as your own private investigator, probing the workings of your mind to figure out what is going on inside its mental walls. Once you sort out some of the patterns that dominate your thinking, you can take your thinking to the next level: you can target those patterns for improvement. You can build on your strengths. You can determine what to retain in your thinking and what to throw out, which of your beliefs are sensible and which are senseless, which are causing problems, which are bringing richness to your life, which are entrapping or limiting you, which are freeing.

No Intellectual Pain, No Intellectual Gain

Although most people readily agree that a *no pain, no gain* attitude is necessary to attain physical fitness, those same people often give up at the first sign of mental discomfort when working on their minds. But if you are unwilling to persevere through intellectual pain, you simply will not develop as a thinker. Without some stress, the condition of the mind, like the body, will not improve. Like it or not, one undeniable fact is *no intellectual pain, no intellectual gain.*

So expect some mental stress, discomfort, and pain as you proceed through this book. When it comes, face it and work through it. Realize that the most important ideas that humans need to learn are often among the most difficult for the mind to understand and accept (like the fact that we are all naturally egocentric). Recognize that the mind, by nature, resists change—especially change that would force it to see itself in an unfavorable light. So, as you begin to internalize the ideas in this book and feel frustrated, uncomfortable, or discouraged, keep pushing forward. Celebrate the fact that you are growing, rather than standing still, like most people. Realize that the reward is in the improved quality of your life that will occur in the long run. You must stretch and work the mind if you want it to become flexible and powerful and if you want it to do the work you need it to do in the many dimensions of your life.

The Twenty-Five-Day Plan

This book introduces twenty-five fundamental ideas about thinking that form the basis of your twenty-five-day plan. We include some of the important ideas we believe people need to grasp if they are to take command of their thinking and their lives. There is nothing magical about the number 25 rather than, say, 30, 24, or 21. And there are always new and important ideas to be learned—ideas that, when internalized and applied, help us think and live better. The development of thinking, you will discover, is an ongoing dynamic process.

We provide the ideas in a twenty-five-day format so that you can get an initial feel for the whole. You also can get an overview and begin to experience the power of ideas aimed at the improvement of thought. As you move through the 25 days, you will realize that you cannot *internalize* any of these ideas in one day. Nevertheless, you can *begin* to bring important and powerful ideas into your thinking and *begin* to practice using them as agents for mental (intellectual) change.

On the first day, you focus on just one idea. On the second day, you focus on a second idea in light of the first. On the third day, you focus on the third idea in light of the second and the first. Each day the tapestry becomes richer. Each day you add a new and powerful idea to your thinking. As you proceed, you will always have a central focus, but your central focus is enriched through the background logic of, and interaction with, other powerful ideas.

As you move from day to day, you should try to integrate previously learned ideas with new ones. Having powerful ideas interact with other powerful ideas is a key to success. Long-term success largely depends on how you proceed after you complete the twenty-five days. Do you keep and use the ideas? Do you forget them? Do you pursue additional important ideas that connect with these ideas? Do you go back to the way you were before you read this book? Do you move forward? These are the kinds of questions you must ask, and revisit again and again, if you want to continue developing as a free and independent thinker.

Use the daily action plans and progress notes in the back of this book to plan and assess your progress as you move through each day.

Expanding to a Twenty-Five-Week Plan

One way to proceed after you work through the *twenty-five-day plan* is to advance to a *twenty-five-week plan*, focusing on one idea per week, rather than one idea per day. In this advanced phase, as you move forward from week to week, you will find the power of each idea being intensified by new interactions with previous ideas. You will begin to see the interrelationships between and among the ideas. Whenever you take important ideas seriously and begin working them into your thinking, you will begin to see that every important idea has many connections to other important ideas. Powerful ideas are powerful *in light of* their important connections.

So we suggest a twenty-five-day sprint to get the ideas flowing. Then a follow-up, longer-term, second run to deepen and further interconnect the ideas and begin to permanently internalize them.

The twenty-five-week plan helps you build good habits of thought as each new idea adds to and connects with ideas learned in previous weeks. For example, following the twenty-five-week plan:

- In the first week you focus on *empathizing with others* whenever and however you can.
- In the second week you concentrate on *uncovering the extent of your ignorance*. (As a matter of second emphasis, though, you should still look for opportunities to *empathize with others*.)
- In the third week you are on the lookout for *hypocrisy*—in yourself and others (while also *empathizing* with others and *uncovering ignorance* in your thinking).

When you have internalized the first three ideas in this book, you will realize that endless problems in thinking occur precisely because people often lack the propensity to empathize, to critique their thinking to differentiate what they know from what they do not know (but assume they know), and to seek out hypocrisy (in themselves and others). Moreover, you should recognize that our propensity to empathize with others increases as we become less intellectually arrogant, less sure that what we think is true must always be true, and, as we become more aware of hypocrisy in our own thinking, more aware of how often we expect more from others than we expect from ourselves.

And so it goes from week to week. Every week you focus on a new and important idea. As you add a new idea, you connect it with ideas already learned.

Periodically you should review all the ideas you have covered and determine whether you need to refresh in your mind one or more of the ideas previously covered. The more often you crisscross the terrain of important and powerful ideas, the more deeply they become embedded in your thinking, and the more likely you are to use them in your life.

In planning and assessing your progress, use the action plans and progress notes at the end of this book.

What is most important, as you expand to a weekly plan, is that at any given time you have a specific focus and that this focus is of sufficient duration. Feel free to move around within the ideas—there is no magic to their order.

When You Reach the Payoff Point

When you have worked through the twenty-five ideas as recommended in this book, applying them on a daily or weekly basis, you should begin to experience payoffs in the quality of your life. The following list outlines some of the payoffs you can expect.

You should find that

- you are better at communicating your ideas and understanding others.
- you are better at sticking to issues and solving problems.
- you pursue more rational goals and can better reach them.
- you are better at asking productive questions.
- you are less selfish.
- you have more control over your emotions.
- you have more control over your desires and behavior.
- you can better understand the viewpoints of others.

- you are more reasonable.
- you are less controlling.
- you are less submissive, less easily intimidated.
- you no longer worry about things you can't do anything about.
- you let go of your emotional baggage from childhood.
- you think through implications before acting.
- you are more comfortable admitting when you are wrong, and you seek to correct your faulty beliefs.
- you work to become a person of integrity, living up to a consistent, rational self-image, and you surround yourself with people of integrity.
- you begin to question social conventions and taboos.
- you begin to question what you read, hear, and see in the news media.
- you are less easily manipulated by smooth-talking, self-interested politicians.
- you are more concerned with the rights and needs of all people in the world, rather than the narrow vested interests of your country.
- you are less easily influenced by TV shows, movies, and ads, viewing them with a more critical eye.
- you are contributing to a more just world.
- you are becoming better educated, reading more widely to broaden your historical sense and your worldview.
- you understand intellectual growth as a long-term process and have designed a plan for continued development.

Tips for Internalizing Each Idea

As you develop your daily or weekly plans for action, consider using one or more of the following strategies:

1. Each evening, read the pages you are focused on for that day. Work the ideas into your thinking (give voice to them) so that you begin to internalize them. Reread the pages until you can engage in a silent dialogue with yourself about the ideas and strategies on those pages.

2. Explain the ideas you are attempting to internalize to someone else. The more you articulate ideas, the better you understand and can use them. (Ideally you would identify someone to work through these ideas with you—a significant other, perhaps).

3. Figure out the best settings for practicing the recommended strategies. Where can you best use them? At work? With your partner? With your children?

4. Think through possible dialogues prior to actual situations. For example, if you are internalizing the idea of clarification (the idea for Day Six), and you plan to be in a meeting on the following day, think through possible clarifying questions. For example, you might prepare to ask "Could you state that point in another way for me?", "Could you give me an example of that?", and "Would you illustrate that point for me by drawing a diagram?"

5. Find ways to keep the key idea of the day in the front of your mind. You might tape a key word (such as "clarity") to the refrigerator, to your desk, or to anything else you frequently see. This will help focus your thinking on the key idea for the day.

Planning and Logging Your Progress

In the back of the book, you will find daily and weekly action plan and progress pages. Copy one set for each day or week, or write in your own notebook or journal (using the action plan and progress formats). The more time you spend giving voice to the ideas (explaining them to others, summarizing them in written form, using them explicitly in your conversations and interactions with others), the better you will internalize them, the more readily and effectively you will be able to use them, and the more spontaneous they will become.

A Caveat

As you work through this book, realize that each day's idea is a complex concept presented in a simplified form. Remember that our goal is to *get you started* on a path toward critical thinking. We therefore have often omitted qualifications and further commentary we would have liked to include. Furthermore, in compressing our ideas, and in seeking examples from everyday life, we may have unwittingly oversimplified some of them. What is more, you may occasionally disagree with one of our examples. If so, try not to be distracted from the larger end: your development as a thinker. Use what you can. Put aside the rest.

If one of our twenty-five ideas does not make sense to you, by all means pass it by and perhaps come back to it later. Give yourself time to grow, and use only those ideas you can put into action. For further explanations of the ideas, you will find recommended readings at the end of the book. We hope these ideas stimulate you to seek more and that they prompt you to make critical thinking a hallmark of your life.

Before You Begin

Before you begin to actively work through the ideas in this book, consider this idea. Then periodically revisit it:

Always assume that you are like other humans. Therefore, expect to find all human failings in yourself.

If humans typically form prejudices, begin with the premise that you have prejudices. If humans frequently engage in self-deception, assume that you do as well. It is impossible to make significant progress as a thinker if you maintain the myth that you are exceptional. The fact is that feeling exceptional is not at all exceptional. It is common. What *is* exceptional is the recognition that you are not exceptional—that you, like everyone else, are a self-deceived, self-centered person.

This is the day to *empathize with others:*

Empathize
Empathize
Empathize

B e on the lookout for opportunities to empathize. Look for examples of empathetic *behavior* in others. Practice being empathetic. For example, whenever someone takes a position with which you disagree, state in your own words what you think the person is saying. Then ask the person whether you have accurately stated her or his position. Notice the extent to which others empathize with you. See whether there is a difference between what they say ("I understand") and what their behavior possibly implies (that they aren't really listening to you). Ask someone who is disagreeing with you to state what he or she understands you to be saying. Notice when people distort what is being said to keep from changing their views or giving up something in their interest. Notice when you do the same. By exercising intellectual empathy, you understand others more fully, expand your knowledge of your own ignorance, and gain deeper insight into your own mind.

Day One:
Learn to Empathize with Others

Intellectual empathy requires us to think within the viewpoints of others, especially those we think are wrong. This is difficult until we recognize how often we have been wrong in the past and others have been right. Those who think differently from us sometimes possess truths we have not yet discovered. Practice in thinking within others' viewpoints is crucial to your development as a thinker. Good thinkers value thinking within opposing viewpoints. They recognize that many truths can be acquired only when they try other ways of thinking. They value gaining new insights and expanding their views. They appreciate new ways of seeing the world. They do not assume that their perspective is the most reasonable one. They are willing to engage in dialog to understand other perspectives. They do not fear ideas and beliefs they do not understand or have never considered. They are ready to abandon beliefs they have passionately held when those beliefs are shown to be false or misleading.

Strategies for empathizing with others:

1. During a disagreement with someone, switch roles. Tell the person, "I will speak from your viewpoint for ten minutes if you will speak from mine. This way perhaps we can understand one another better." Afterward, each of you should correct the other's representation of your position: "The part of my position you don't understand is...."

2. During a discussion, summarize what another person is saying using this structure: "What I understand you to be saying is.... Is this correct?"

3. When reading, say to yourself what you think the author is saying. Explain it to someone else. Recheck the text for accuracy. This enables you to assess your understanding of an author's viewpoint. Only when you are sure you understand a viewpoint are you in a position to disagree (or agree) with it.

"HE WHO LIVES IN IGNORANCE OF OTHERS LIVES IN IGNORANCE OF HIMSELF."
—ANONYMOUS

This is the day to *discover your ignorance:*

Discover Your Ignorance

Discover Your Ignorance

Be on the lookout for intellectual arrogance, the tendency to confidently assert as true what you do not in fact know to be true. Try to discover the limitations and biases of your sources of information. Question those who speak with authority. Question the information they use in their arguments, the information they ignore, the information they distort. Question what you read and see in the media. Notice the confidence with which The News is asserted. Question the sources that "produce" the news. Whenever you feel inclined to make a bold statement, stop and ask how much you really know about what you're asserting.

Day Two:
Develop Knowledge of Your Ignorance

Most of us assume that whatever we believe must be right. Though we were taught much of what we believe before we could critically analyze our beliefs, we nevertheless defend our beliefs as *the truth*. Good thinkers know this is absurd.

When you actively focus on uncovering your ignorance, you realize that you are often wrong. You look for opportunities to test your ideas for soundness. You recognize that much of what people believe is based on prejudice, bias, half-truths, and sometimes even superstition. You routinely question your beliefs. Your beliefs do not control you; you control your beliefs. You develop intellectual humility—awareness of the extent of your ignorance.

Intellectual humility is the disposition to distinguish, at any given moment and in any given situation, between what you know and what you don't. People disposed toward intellectual humility recognize the natural tendency of the mind to think it knows more than it does, to see itself as right when the evidence proves otherwise. They routinely think within alternative viewpoints, making sure they are accurately representing those viewpoints. They enter other viewpoints to understand them, rather than to dismiss them.

Socrates, an early Greek philosopher and teacher (c. 470–399 B.C.), was a living model of intellectual humility. Consider:

> *"Socrates philosophized by joining in a discussion with another person who thought he knew what justice, courage, or the like was. Under Socrates' questioning it became clear that neither [of the two] knew, and they cooperated in a new effort, Socrates making interrogatory suggestions that were accepted or rejected by his friend. They failed to solve the problem, but, now conscious of their lack of knowledge, agreed to continue the search whenever possible (p. 483)."* [3]

---

[3] Encyclopedia of Philosophy, 1972.

"Profoundly sensible of the inconsistencies of his own thoughts and words and actions, and shrewdly suspecting that the like inconsistencies were to be found in other men, he was careful always to place himself upon the standpoint of ignorance and to invite others to join him there, in order that, proving all things, he and they might hold fast to that which is good (p. 332)." [4]

People with intellectual humility (and they are rare) understand that there is far more that they will *never* know than they will *ever* know. They continually seek to learn more, to develop their intellectual abilities and expand their knowledge base, always with a healthy awareness of the limits of their knowledge.

Strategies for developing intellectual humility:

1. When you cannot find sufficient evidence that *proves* your belief to be true, begin by saying: "I may be wrong, but what I think is..." or "Up to this point I have believed..." or "Based on my limited knowledge in this area, I would say...".

2. Notice when you argue for beliefs without evidence to justify them. Recognize why you are doing this.

3. Actively question beliefs that seem obviously true to you, especially deeply held beliefs such as religious, cultural, or political beliefs.

4. Find alternative sources of information that represent viewpoints you have never considered.

5. Don't be afraid to "explore" new beliefs, and hence to be open to new insights.

6. Make a list of everything you absolutely know about someone you think you know well. Then make a list of things you think are true about that person, but that you cannot be absolutely sure about. Then make a list of things you do not know about that person. Then, if you can trust the person, show him or her your list to see how accurate you are. What insights emerge for you after you get feedback on such lists?

---

[4] Encyclopedia Britannica, Eleventh Edition, 1911.

Questions you might ask to identify weaknesses in your thinking:

- What do I really know (about myself, about this or that situation, about another person, about my nation, about what is going on in the world)?
- To what extent do my prejudices or biases influence my thinking?
- To what extent have I been indoctrinated into beliefs that might be false?
- How do the beliefs I have accepted uncritically keep me from seeing things as they are?
- Do I ever think outside the box (of my culture, nation, religion...)?
- How knowledgeable am I about alternative belief systems?
- How have my beliefs been shaped by the time period in which I was born, by the place in which I was raised, by my parents' beliefs, by my spouse's beliefs, by my religion, culture, politics, and so on?

"WILLINGNESS TO BE TAUGHT WHAT WE DO NOT KNOW IS THE SURE PLEDGE OF GROWTH BOTH IN KNOWLEDGE AND WISDOM."
—BLAIR

This is the day for *integrity:*

Don't Be a Hypocrite

Don't Be a Hypocrite

B e on the lookout for contradictions or hypocrisy in your behavior and the behavior of others. Catch yourself using double standards. Notice when others do. Because hypocrisy is a natural human tendency, theoretically this should be easy. Look closely at what people say they believe. Compare this with what their behavior implies. Dig out inconsistencies in your thinking and behavior. Notice when you profess a belief, and then act in contradiction to that belief. Notice how you justify or rationalize inconsistencies in your behavior. Figure out the consequence of your hypocrisy. Does it enable you to get what you want without having to face the truth about yourself? Figure out the consequences of others' hypocrisy. However, if you don't see hypocrisy in yourself, look again and again and again.

Day Three:
Beware of Hypocrisy;
Notice Contradictions in Your Life

People are hypocritical in at least three ways. First, they tend to have higher standards for those with whom they disagree than they have for themselves or their friends. Second, they often fail to live in accordance with their professed beliefs. Third, they often fail to see contradictions in the behavior of people with high status.

Hypocrisy, then, is a state of mind unconcerned with honesty. It is often marked by unconscious contradictions and inconsistencies. Because the mind is naturally egocentric, it is naturally hypocritical. Yet at the same time, it can skillfully rationalize whatever it thinks and does. In other words, the human mind naturally wants to see itself in a positive light. The *appearance* of integrity is important to the egocentric mind. This is why, as humans, we actively hide our hypocrisy from ourselves and others. And although we expect others to adhere to much more rigid standards than the standards we impose on ourselves, we see ourselves as fair. Though we profess certain beliefs, we often fail to behave in accordance with those beliefs.

Only to the extent that our beliefs and actions are consistent, only when we say what we mean and mean what we say, do we have intellectual integrity.

When you resolve to live a life of integrity, you routinely examine your own inconsistencies and face them truthfully, without excuses. You want to know the truth about yourself. You want to know the truth in others. By facing your own hypocrisy, you begin to grow beyond it (while recognizing that you can never get full command of your hypocrisy because you can never get full command of your egocentricity). When you recognize it in others (especially those of status), they are less able to manipulate you.

Strategies for reducing hypocrisy in yourself:

1. Begin to notice situations in which you expect more from others than you do from yourself. Pin down the areas of your greatest hypocrisy (these are usually areas in which you are emotionally involved). Do you expect more from your spouse than you do from yourself? From your coworkers? From your subordinates? From your children?

2. Make a list of beliefs that seem most important to you. Then identify situations in which your behavior is inconsistent with those beliefs (where you say one thing and do another). Realize that what you really believe is embedded in that which you do, not that which you say. What does your behavior tell you about yourself? (For example, you might say that you love someone while often failing to behave in accordance with his or her interests.)

Strategies for noticing hypocrisy in others:

1. Observe the people around you. Begin to analyze the extent to which they say one thing and do another. Compare their words to their deeds. For example, notice how often people claim to love someone they criticize behind the person's back. This is a common form of bad faith.

2. Think about the people you are closest to—your partner, spouse, children, or friends. To what extent can you identify hypocrisy or integrity in those relationships? To what extent do they say what they mean and mean what they say? What problems are caused by their hypocrisy?

"WE ARE COMPANIONS IN HYPOCRISY."
—WILLIAM DEAN HOWELLS

This is the day to *catch yourself being selfish:*

Catch Yourself Being Selfish

Catch Yourself Being Selfish

B e on the lookout for selfishness—in yourself and others. Notice how often people justify their selfishness. Notice how often they object to the selfishness of others. Look closely at the role of selfishness in your life. Note how hard it is to be fair to those you have been taught to consider "evil." Note how difficult it is to identify your own unfair behavior (because the mind naturally hides what it doesn't want to face).

Day Four:
Be Fair, Not Selfish

Human thinking is naturally self-serving or selfish. Selfishness is a *native*, not learned, human tendency (though it can be encouraged or discouraged by one's culture). Humans naturally tend to look out for "number one." Unfortunately, that often means we are unfair to persons "two" and "three."

You don't have to be selfish. It is possible to develop as a fair person and thinker. You can learn to give significant attention to the desires, needs, and rights of others. You need not "cheat yourself" to be fair.

When you think fair-mindedly, you consider the rights and needs of others as equivalent to your own. You forego the pursuit of your desires when fair play requires it. You learn how to overcome your selfishness. You learn how to step outside your point of view and into others' points of view. You value fair-mindedness as a personal characteristic worth pursuing.

Strategies for developing as a fair-minded thinker:

1. Recognize anew, every day, that you, like every other human, are *naturally* self-centered—that you, like every other human, are primarily interested in how the world and everything in it can serve you. Only by bringing this idea to the forefront of your thinking can you begin to get command of your selfishness and self-centered tendencies.

2. Be on the alert to catch yourself in the mental act of self-deception—for example, ignoring others' viewpoints. Remember that all humans engage in some self-deception. The exceptional persons are those who recognize this tendency in themselves and consistently work to take command of it.

3. Log each time you do something selfish. Try to see past the rationalizations your mind uses to justify its self-serving behavior. Write down in detail how and when you are selfish. Then write down the point of view of those who are affected by your selfishness. Consider how you can avoid such behavior in future similar situations. You might use the following format to log your selfish episodes:

    a. Today I was selfish in the following way...

      b. My selfish (but unspoken) thinking was as follows... (Be as honest as possible. Do not allow your mind to get away with self-deception as you detail your thinking.)

      c. My selfishness affected the following person or people in the following way(s)...

      d. In the future, I can avoid being selfish or self-centered in a similar situation by thinking and behaving in the following rational ways...

4. Take every opportunity you can to think broadly about issues that involve multiple viewpoints. Assume that your mind will tend to favor whatever perspective you hold in any given situation. Force your mind, if necessary, to consider other relevant ways of looking at the issue or situation (and to represent those viewpoints accurately, rather than in a distorted way).

Questions you can ask to foster fairness in your thinking:

- Am I being fair to...right now?

- Am I putting my *desires* ahead of the *rights* and *needs* of others? If so, what precisely am I after, and whose rights or needs am I ignoring or violating?

- When I think about the way I live, how often do I put myself in others' shoes?

- Do I have a selfish interest in not seeing the truth in this situation? If I face the truth, will I have to change my behavior?

- Do I think broadly enough to be fair? How many alternative perspectives have I explored? What national, religious, political, ideological, and social points of view have I considered?

- In what types of situations do I tend to be selfish? With my spouse? My children? My friends? At work?

"SELFISHNESS IS THAT DETESTABLE VICE WHICH NO ONE WILL FORGIVE IN OTHERS, AND NO ONE IS WITHOUT IN HIMSELF."
–H.W. BEECHER

This is the day to *target purposes:*

Empathize with Others
Uncover Your Ignorance
Notice Contradictions
Be Fair, Not Selfish
Stick to Your Purpose
Be Clear
Be Relevant
Question, Question, Question
Think Through Implications
Control Your Emotions
Control Your Desires
Be Reasonable
Show Mercy
Think for Yourself
Don't Be a Top Dog
Don't Be an Underdog
Don't Be a Worry Wart
Stop Blaming Your Parents
Critique the News Media
See Through Politicians
Be a Citizen of the World
Notice Media Garbage
Make Your Mark
Educate Yourself
Figure Out Where to Go

Target Purposes

Target Purposes

Target Purposes

Be on the lookout for goals, purposes, objectives, agendas. Figure out what you are after and how you are seeking it. Determine whether your various goals are interwoven and convergent or in conflict and mutually inconsistent. Determine whether your real purposes are different from your expressed purposes. Ask yourself whether you can admit your real purposes (in this or that part of your life). Figure out what your family members, associates, and friends are after. What are their real and most basic goals? To what extent are their lives undermined by contradictory drives and aims? To what extent can they admit their real purposes? Examine personal goals, professional goals, political goals, economic goals, national goals. Make a list of your important goals and see if you find inconsistencies in them.

Day Five:
Know Your Purpose

Thinking is always guided by human purposes. Everything you do is related to some purpose you have. Your purpose is whatever you are trying to accomplish. It is your goal or objective in any given situation or context.

Your thinking goes wrong when you aren't clear about your purpose, have unrealistic purposes, have contradictory purposes, or don't stick to your expressed purpose. Some goals are short-range and transitory; others are long-range and permanent. Some are primary. Some are secondary. Some represent your central mission in life. Others become means to other ends.

In human life, there is often a discrepancy between public (announced) goals and private (unspoken) goals. Thus, a politician's *announced* goal is usually to serve public need. The *real* goal is often to get elected, to serve ambition, and to satisfy greed.

It is important to examine the purposes that guide how you live. Which of them are you explicitly aware of? Which of them lie beneath the surface of your thinking? Which of them would you be unwilling to admit to? How many of them guide you to superficial actions? How many of them guide you to important ends? Which of them are you having difficulty accomplishing, and why?

It is also important to be able to assess others' purposes. Remembering that people's real purposes often contradict their stated purposes will enable you to see through façades and keep from being manipulated by others.

Questions you can ask to target purpose:

- What exactly is my purpose in this situation?
- What am I trying to accomplish?
- Is this purpose realistic?
- Is this goal ethically justified?
- What is my most important task right now?
- What is the first thing I need to do to accomplish my purpose?
- What is the agenda of my spouse, my children, my friends?

- How does my agenda differ from my spouse's, employee's, or supervisor's?
- Does my stated agenda differ from my actual one?
- Would I be willing to admit to my true purpose in this situation? If not, why not?

"THERE IS NO ROAD TO SUCCESS BUT THROUGH A CLEAR STRONG PURPOSE. NOTHING CAN TAKE ITS PLACE. A PURPOSE UNDERLIES CHARACTER, CULTURE, POSITION, ATTAINMENT OF EVERY SORT."
—T.T. MUNGER

This is the day to *be clear:*

Clarify

Clarify

Clarify

Be on the lookout for vague, fuzzy, blurred thinking—thinking that may sound good but that doesn't really say anything. Try to figure out the real meaning of what people are saying. Look on the surface. Look beneath the surface. Try to figure out the real meaning of important news stories. Explain your understanding of an issue to someone else to help clarify it in your own mind. Practice summarizing in your own words what others say. Then ask them if you understood them correctly. Be careful to neither agree nor disagree with what anyone says until you (clearly) understand what he or she is saying.

Day Six:
Clarify Your Thinking

Our own thinking usually seems clear to us, even when it is not. Vague, ambiguous, muddled, deceptive, or misleading thinking are significant problems in human life. If you are to develop as a thinker, you must learn the art of clarifying thinking—of pinning it down, spelling it out, and giving it a specific meaning. Here's what you can do to begin. When people explain things to you, summarize in your own words what you think they said. When you cannot do this to their satisfaction, you don't really understand what they said. When they cannot summarize to your satisfaction what you have said, they don't really understand what you said. Try it. See what happens.

Strategies for clarifying your thinking:

To improve your ability to clarify your thinking (in your own mind, when speaking to others, when writing), you can do some very basic things:

1. State one point at a time.
2. Elaborate on what you mean.
3. Give examples that connect your thoughts to life experiences.
4. Use analogies and metaphors to help people connect your ideas to a variety of things they already understand. (Consider this analogy: Critical thinking is like an onion. It has many layers. Just when you think you have it basically figured out, you realize there is another layer, and then another, and another and another and on and on.)

Here is one format you can use to make sure you are clear when speaking or writing your thoughts:

- I think... (state your main point)
- In other words... (elaborate on your main point)
- For example... (give an example of your main point)
- To give you an analogy... (give an illustration of your main point)

To clarify other people's thinking, you might ask any of the following questions:

- Can you restate your point in other words? I didn't understand you.
- Can you give an example?
- Let me tell you what I understand you to be saying. Do I understand you correctly?

As you begin to use these strategies, note how seldom others use them. Begin to notice how often people assume that others understand them when what they have said is, in fact, unintelligible, muddy, or confusing. Note how, very often, the *simple* intellectual moves are the most powerful. (For example, simply say to someone: "I don't understand what you are saying. Can you say that in other words?") Focus on using these basic, foundational moves whenever it seems at all relevant to do so. As you do, you will find that your thinking becomes clearer and clearer, and you get better and better at clarifying others' thinking.

**"MUDDLED THINKING IS THE FIRST STEP
ON THE ROAD TO A MUDDLED LIFE."
—ANONYMOUS**

This is the day to be relevant:

Focus, Connect, Stick to the Point

Be on the lookout for fragmented thinking—thinking that leaps about with no logical connections. Start noticing when you or others fail to stay focused on what is relevant. Focus on finding what will help you solve a problem. When someone brings up a point that doesn't seem pertinent to the issue at hand, ask: "How is what you're saying relevant to the issue?" When you are working through a problem, make sure you stay focused on what sheds light on, and thus helps address, the problem. Don't allow your mind to wander to unrelated matters. Don't allow others to stray from the main issue or divert you. Frequently ask: "What is the central question? Is this or that relevant to it? How?"

Day Seven:
Stick to the Point

When thinking is relevant, it is focused on the main task at hand.

It selects what is germane, pertinent, related. It is on the alert for everything that connects to the issue. It sets aside what is immaterial, inappropriate, extraneous, beside the point. That which directly bears upon (helps solve) the problem you are trying to solve is *relevant* to the problem. When thinking drifts away from what is relevant, it needs to be brought back to what truly makes a difference. Undisciplined thinking is often guided by associations (this reminds me of that, that reminds me of this other thing) rather than what is logically connected ("If a and b are true, c must also be true"). Disciplined thinking intervenes when thoughts wander and concentrates the mind on the things that help it figure out what it needs to figure out.

If you find your thinking digressing, try to figure out why. Is your mind simply wandering? If so, you probably need to intervene to get it back on track. Or perhaps you realize that you need to deal with a different issue before addressing the one you were originally focused on. If so, by all means address the issue your mind has surfaced. But most importantly, *know precisely, at any given moment, the issue you are addressing*. And then stick to that issue until you have either reached resolution or made an active decision to revisit the issue later, or deal with the alternative issue that has emerged and stick to that issue. But do not allow your mind to wander aimlessly from idea to idea, issue to issue, without direction or discipline.

Questions you can ask to make sure your thinking is focused on what is relevant:

- Am I focused on the main problem or task?
- How are these two issues connected, or are they?
- How is the problem I have raised intertwined with the issue at hand?
- Does the information I am considering directly relate to the problem or task?
- Where do I need to focus my attention?

- Am I being diverted to unrelated matters?
- Am I failing to consider relevant viewpoints?
- How is my point relevant to the issue I am addressing?
- What facts will actually help me answer the question? What considerations should be set aside?
- Does this truly bear on the question? How does it connect?

"IF WE ARE TO SOLVE A PROBLEM, WE MUST PURSUE IT WITH ALL OUR INTELLECTUAL PROWESS, IDENTIFYING EXACTLY THAT WHICH HELPS US SOLVE IT, AND WEEDING OUT THAT WHICH GETS IN THE WAY."
—ANONYMOUS

This is the day to *ask deep questions:*

Question

Question

Question

Empathize with Others
Uncover Your Ignorance
Notice Contradictions
Be Fair, Not Selfish
Stick to Your Purpose
Be Clear
Be Relevant
Question, Question, Question
Think Through Implications
Control Your Emotions
Control Your Desires
Be Reasonable
Show Mercy
Think for Yourself
Don't Be a Top Dog
Don't Be an Underdog
Don't Be a Worry Wart
Stop Blaming Your Parents
Critique the News Media
See Through Politicians
Be a Citizen of the World
Notice Media Garbage
Make Your Mark
Educate Yourself
Figure Out Where to Go

B e on the lookout for questions. Look closely at the questions you and others ask. What *types* of questions do you tend to ask? When do you fail to ask important and relevant questions? Do you tend to ask deep questions or superficial ones? Listen to how others question, when they question, when they fail to question. Examine the extent to which you are a questioner, or simply one who accepts definitions of situations given by others. Focus on bringing your mind alive by improving the quality of the questions you ask. Notice the questions that guide your actions. Notice the questions that guide the actions of others.

Day Eight:
Question, Question, Question

Thinking is driven by questions. The quality of your questions determines the quality of your thinking. Superficial questions lead to superficial thinking. Deep questions lead to deep thinking. Insightful questions lead to insightful thinking. Creative questions lead to creative thinking.

Moreover, questions determine the intellectual tasks required of you—if you are to answer them sufficiently. (For example, the question "Are there any apples in the refrigerator?" implies that, to answer the question, you need to look in the refrigerator. The question "What is the best way to parent in this situation?" calls on you to think about the concept of parenting, to think about the specific parenting issues you are facing at the moment, to think about the options available to you.) Thus, questions lay out different, but specific, tasks for the mind to work through.

Good thinkers routinely ask questions to understand and effectively deal with the world around them. They question the status quo. They know that things are often different from how they are presented. Their questions penetrate images, masks, fronts, and propaganda. Their questions bring clarity and precision to the problems they face. Their questions bring discipline to their thinking. Their questions show that they do not necessarily accept the world as it is presented to them. They go beyond superficial or "loaded" questions. Their questions help them solve their problems and make better decisions.

When you become a student of questions, you learn to ask powerful questions that lead to a deeper and more fulfilling life. Your questions become more basic, essential, and deep. When you understand the questions other people are asking, you can better understand their thinking and viewpoint.

Strategies for formulating more powerful questions:

1. Whenever you don't understand something, ask a question to clarify precisely what you do not understand. Never answer a question unless you understand what it is asking.

2. Whenever you are dealing with a complex problem, formulate the question you are trying to answer in several different ways (being as precise as you can) until you hit on the way that best addresses

the problem at hand. Then figure out what issues, problems, or ideas you need to think through to answer the question. Figure out what information you need to consider. Do you need to look at the question from multiple viewpoints? If so, detail those viewpoints as clearly and accurately as possible before proceeding to answer the question.

3. Whenever you plan to discuss an important issue or problem, write down in advance the most significant questions you need to address in the discussion. Be ready to change the main question if necessary. As soon as the question is clear, help those in the discussion stick to the question, making sure that the dialogue builds toward an answer that makes sense.

Questions you can ask to discipline your thinking:

- What precise question am I trying to answer?
- Is that the best question to ask in this situation?
- Is there a more important question I should be addressing?
- Does this question capture the real issue I am facing?
- Is there a question I should answer before I attempt to answer this question?
- What information do I need to gather to answer the question?
- What conclusions seem justified in light of the facts?
- What is my point of view? Do I need to consider another?
- Is there another way to look at the question?
- What are some related questions I need to consider?
- What type of question is this: an economic question, a political question, a legal question, an ethical question, a complex question with multiple domains?

"'HOW DO YOU KNOW SO MUCH ABOUT EVERYTHING?' WAS ASKED OF A VERY WISE AND INTELLIGENT MAN; AND THE ANSWER WAS, 'BY NEVER BEING AFRAID OR ASHAMED TO ASK QUESTIONS AS TO ANYTHING OF WHICH I WAS IGNORANT.'"
–J. ABBOTT

This is the day to *think through implications:*

Implications

Implications

Implications

Empathize with Others
Uncover Your Ignorance
Notice Contradictions
Be Fair, Not Selfish
Stick to Your Purpose
Be Clear
Be Relevant
Question, Question, Question
Think Through Implications
Control Your Emotions
Control Your Desires
Be Reasonable
Show Mercy
Think for Yourself
Don't Be a Top Dog
Don't Be an Underdog
Don't Be a Worry Wart
Stop Blaming Your Parents
Critique the News Media
See Through Politicians
Be a Citizen of the World
Notice Media Garbage
Make Your Mark
Educate Yourself
Figure Out Where to Go

B e on the lookout for implications of decisions or potential decisions—your decisions, others' decisions.

Look on the surface for obvious implications. Look beneath the surface for less-obvious implications. Notice the implications of what you say. Look closely at the consequences of your actions. Make a list of all the significant implications of a potential decision before acting. Notice when others fail to think through implications. Look for examples in the newspaper. Notice that some decisions have insignificant results. Notice that others (such as a decision to go to war) lead to deadly results and ruined lives. Look for opportunities to help others think through implications (your children or your significant other, for example).

Day Nine:
Think Through Implications

Implications are the things that *might* happen if you decide to do this or that. Consequences are the things that *actually* happen once you act. When you consider the implications of what you might do before you do it, you explicitly choose (insofar as you can) the consequences that happen when you act. Some people simply don't imagine what will or might follow when they act on a decision they have made. They smoke but are unprepared for lung problems. They don't exercise but are unprepared for muscle deterioration. They don't actively develop their minds but are unprepared for the increasing inflexibility and close-mindedness that come with aging when one does not actively "work" the mind. They don't realize that everything they do has implications. They don't realize that it is possible to make a habit of thinking through the implications of decisions *before* acting, and thus learn to act more wisely, to live more rationally. Critical, reflective thinkers actively consider the implications of their actions before acting and modify their behavior accordingly (before they experience negative consequences).

Not only are there implications for our decisions, but implications are embedded in what we say, in the words we decide to use. Put another way, the way we use language implies certain specific things. For example, if you say to your wife, in a loud and angry tone, "Why the hell didn't you do the dishes?", you imply, at a minimum:

- She should have done the dishes.
- She knows that she should have done the dishes.
- She knew you would be upset if she didn't do them.
- In the future, under similar circumstances, she had better do the dishes unless she wants you to be angry with her.

Because implications are connected with or follow from everything you say, choose your words carefully. Before you say anything, be sure you have thought through the implications of your words. Resolve to use language with care and precision.

Strategies for thinking through implications:

1. Look at your life as a set of moment-to-moment options. At any moment, you can do X or Y or Z. Each and every act, and every pattern of actions, has outcomes. What outcomes do you want?

What must you do to anticipate likely outcomes? (The answer is, become a student of your own behavior, reflect on the likely outcomes of possible decisions, and make your decisions more mindfully.)

2. When faced with a difficult problem, make a list of the likely implications of dealing with the problem in various ways. Then act in the way that is likely to lead to the outcome you want.

3. Think about the implications (for future health and happiness) of the way you are now living your life. Make a list of the implications you probably will face for continuing to live as you are. Will you be satisfied with those implications? Think especially hard about the likely negative implications of your habits.

4. Carefully observe the language you choose to use when framing your thoughts. Note what is implied by what you say. (Note also what is implied by what others say.) Notice how others react to what you say to them. Make a commitment to carefully choose your words before speaking to others (so as to be aware of what you may imply).

Questions you should ask to target implications:

- If I decide to do X, what is likely to happen?
- If I decide not to do X, what is likely to happen?
- If we make this decision in this relationship, what are the implications? What were the consequences when we made similar decisions before?
- What are the implications of ignoring this or that problem (for example, in an important relationship or in parenting)?
- If I keep living in the present as I have in the past, what consequences will I likely face?

"FOOLS MEASURE ACTIONS AFTER THEY ARE DONE,
BY THE EVENT; WISE MEN BEFOREHAND,
BY THE RULES OF REASON."
—RICHARD HILL

This is the day to *get control of your emotions:*

Check Your Emotions

Check Your Emotions

Take special note of feelings and emotions. Your emotions. The emotions of others. Look on the surface, at the emotions you are aware of. Look beneath the surface, for the emotions you would deny you feel. Notice how people often justify their own negative emotions. Notice how they often object to the negative emotions of others. Notice how we tend to invalidate the emotions of those we consider beneath us, or those whose views we do not share. Look closely at the role of emotions in your life. Realize that even negative emotions can serve a useful role in your development. If you are doing things to hurt others, you *should* feel bad about what you are doing. Do not confuse the feelings of a healthy conscience with the emotions of egocentricity. Every time you feel a negative emotion, stop and ask yourself: Why? What thoughts or behavior are leading to this feeling? Resolve to attack unproductive thinking with productive thinking—leading to productive feelings.

Day Ten:
Get Control of Your Emotions

People are often confused about the role of emotions in life. For example, they sometimes place people in one of two categories: thinkers or feelers. As a result, they might make the following kind of statement: "The problem in our relationship is that you are a thinker and I feel things. I am an emotional person. You aren't." But differentiating between *thinkers* and *feelers* is a conceptual mistake. As humans, all of us think, and all of us experience emotions throughout the day, every day.

Thoughts and feelings are two sides of the same coin. If you *think*, for example, that someone has been unjust to you, you will *feel* some negative emotion (such as anger or resentment) toward that person. The feeling *happens* in the mind as a result of how you think in the situation. Moreover, feelings can usefully influence and drive thought. For example, if you are angry about something you think is unjust, your anger can drive you to think about what you can do to eliminate the injustice.

Feelings and emotions, then, are an important part of your life. They can be positive or negative. They signal whether you are perceiving things in a positive or negative light. They can be justified or unjustified. How you relate to your emotions can make a big difference in the quality of your life. You can feed or starve your emotions. You can use your emotions effectively or ineffectively. As you learn to examine your emotions, investigate the thinking that accounts for them. You can attack thinking that leads to self-inflicted unproductive emotional pain. You can take command of your emotions by taking command of the thinking that causes those emotions.

Strategies for taking command of your emotional life:

1. Begin to notice the emotions you regularly experience. Every time you experience a negative emotion, ask yourself: What thinking is leading to this emotion? See if you can identify some irrational thinking underlying the emotion. If so, attack that thinking with better, more sensible thinking. Once you act on the new thinking, your emotion should begin to shift accordingly.

2. If you experience negative emotions frequently in your life, look closely at what is causing these emotions. Is it you? Is your irrational thinking leading to unproductive behavior? Are you in a dysfunctional relationship that you need to get out of? Is it your job? Until you directly face the problems in your life that are causing negative emotions, and until you do something to change the situation, the negative emotions will keep coming back. Get to the root of the emotions. Attack your mind with thinking that leads to productive behavior and positive emotions.

3. To focus more concretely on your emotions, write about them. Keep a daily journal that targets the negative emotions you experience. Use this format:

   a. One negative emotion I feel is...

   b. The reason I feel this negative emotion is...

   c. The thinking (or situation) I need to change in order not to feel this negative emotion is...

   d. A more productive way to think is, If I change the way I think, my feelings should change in the following ways...

The focus in this strategy is on negative emotions. By analyzing what is giving rise to negative emotions, you can often identify problems in your thinking and behavior. If you don't experience many negative emotions, there can be a number of reasons why. For example, it may be that you are living a predominantly rational life, and therefore you experience the positive emotions that come with reasonable, unselfish living. Or it may be that you can get what you want without regard for the rights and needs of others. For example, the successful dominator primarily feels positive emotions (see Day 15, "Don't Be a Top Dog"). It is up to you to determine the truth about your emotional life.

"EMOTION TURNING BACK ON ITSELF, AND NOT LEADING ON TO THOUGHT OR ACTION, IS AN ELEMENT OF MADNESS..."
—J. STERLING

This is the day to *take control of your desires:*

Check Your Desires

Empathize with Others
Uncover Your Ignorance
Notice Contradictions
Be Fair, Not Selfish
Stick to Your Purpose
Be Clear
Be Relevant
Question, Question, Question
Think Through Implications
Control Your Emotions
Control Your Desires
Be Reasonable
Show Mercy
Think for Yourself
Don't Be a Top Dog
Don't Be an Underdog
Don't Be a Worry Wart
Stop Blaming Your Parents
Critique the News Media
See Through Politicians
Be a Citizen of the World
Notice Media Garbage
Make Your Mark
Educate Yourself
Figure Out Where to Go

Check Your Desires

B e on the lookout for desires. Your desires. The desires of others. Notice how often people pursue irrational desires. Seek to identify which of your desires you can admit and which you try to hide. Notice how often people try to justify self-serving desires. Notice how they object to the self-serving desires of others. Look closely at the implications of desires in your life. Every pursuit has its price. Notice how the pursuit of wealth, power, status, and celebrity impacts the quality of life—for you and others. Much suffering and injustice result from them. You can never be a reasonable or just person if you are subservient to selfish or irrational desires.

Day Eleven:
Take Control of Your Desires

If you want to be in command of your life, you have to get command of the desires that direct your behavior. Otherwise, it is all too easy to pursue irrational desires—desires that are self-destructive or harmful to others, such as the desire to dominate. When you don't actively assess and critique what you want, you often end up pursuing senseless desires without knowing why.

But when you develop as a self-reflective thinker, you can differentiate between desires that make sense and those that don't, between those that can be justified and those that cannot. You work to reject desires that lead to suffering. You break down habits that feed self-destructive desires. You establish habits conducive to a fulfilling life. Recognizing that much suffering results from the unbridled pursuits of greed, power, or approval, you carefully monitor these natural, but harmful, human desires in yourself. You simplify your life. Realizing that most irrational desires function at the unconscious level of thought, you work to bring unconscious desires to the conscious level. You formulate your purposes, goals, and motives explicitly so that you can assess them.

It is important to realize that desires function in relation to thoughts and feelings. Wherever you have desires, you have thinking leading to those desires. And you experience feelings when you act on those desires. For example, if you desire, or *want*, to move to a different job, you *think* that the job will be better than your current job in one or more ways. When you begin working at the new job, you then *feel* some emotions as a result (satisfaction, dissatisfaction, fulfillment, or frustration, for example). If you *feel* dissatisfied, you may be *driven* to *rethink* your decision. You may try to go back to your old job. And so it goes.

Thus, each of the mind's three functions—thoughts, feelings, and emotions—continually interact and influence one another. Critical thinkers understand the relationship between thoughts, feelings, and desires. They routinely assess the desires guiding their behavior. They analyze the thinking that gives rise to those desires.

Strategies for controlling your desires:

1. Recognize that every action you take is driven by some purpose or desire you have. Make a list of every behavior you engage in that leads to humiliation, pain, or suffering, or that is dysfunctional in some other way (to yourself or others). For every behavior on your list, write a detailed explanation of why you engage in this behavior. Question each. What motivates you?

2. Think through the implications of each behavior you just listed. Detail in writing what happens, or might happen, as a result of each behavior. Be as specific as possible. Don't hide from the truth.

3. List some things you can do immediately to alter your dysfunctional behavior (remember that your behavior comes from your desires). Your behavior is probably influenced by your situation. Reflect. Do you need to change some things in your situation? Do you need to move? Do you need to get out of a bad relationship? Do you need to get help from a professional? Do you need to learn better coping strategies?

4. Write down a detailed plan for changing your dysfunctional behavior. The more details, the more useful your plan will be.

"NO MAN IS FREE WHO CANNOT CONTROL HIMSELF."
—PYTHAGORAS

This is the day to *be reasonable:*

Be Reasonable

Be Reasonable

Be Reasonable

Be on the lookout for reasonable and unreasonable behaviors—yours and others'. Notice when you are unwilling to listen to the reasoned views of others, when you are unwilling to modify your views even when others present evidence or good reasoning supporting a better view. Carefully observe yourself. Can you be moved by reason? Are you open to the voice of reason in others? When you catch yourself being defensive, see if you can break through your defensiveness to hear good reasons being presented. Identify times when you use language that makes you appear reasonable, even though your behavior proves otherwise. Try to figure out why you, or others, are being unreasonable. Might you have a selfish interest in not being open-minded? Might they?

Day Twelve:
Be Reasonable

One of the hallmarks of a critical thinker is the disposition to change one's mind when given a good reason to change. Good thinkers want to change their thinking when they discover better thinking. In other words, they can be *moved* by reason.

Yet, comparatively few people are reasonable in the full sense of the word. Few are willing to change their minds once set. Few are willing to suspend their beliefs to hear the views of those with whom they disagree. This is true because the human mind is not *naturally* reasonable. Reasonability, if it is to develop in the mind to any significant degree, must be actively fostered in the mind by the mind. Although we routinely make inferences or come to conclusions, we don't necessarily do so *reasonably*. Yet we typically see our conclusions as reasonable. We then want to *stick to our conclusions* without regard for their justification or plausibility. In short, the mind typically decides whether to accept or reject a viewpoint or argument based on *whether it already believes it*.

To put it another way, the mind is not naturally malleable. Rather, the mind is, by nature, *rigid*. It often shuts out good reasons readily available to it. It often refuses to hear arguments that are perfectly reasonable (when those reasons contradict what it already believes).

To become more reasonable, you need to open your mind to the possibility, at any given moment, that you might be wrong and another person may be right. You need to be willing and able to change your mind when the situation or evidence requires it. You need to recognize that you don't lose anything by admitting that you are wrong. Rather, you gain.

Strategies for becoming more reasonable:

1. Notice how seldom people admit they are wrong. Notice, instead, how often they hide their mistakes. Most people would rather lie than admit to being wrong. Decide that you do not want to be such a person.

2. Say aloud: "I'm not perfect. I make mistakes. I'm often wrong." See if you have the courage to admit this during a disagreement: "Of course, I may be wrong. You may be right."

3. Practice saying in your own mind, "I may be wrong. I often am. I'm willing to change my mind when given good reasons." Then look for opportunities to make changes in your thinking.

4. Ask yourself, "When was the last time I changed my mind because someone gave me better reasons for his or her views than I had for mine?" To what extent are you open to new ways of looking at things? To what extent can you objectively judge information that refutes what you already think?

5. Realize that you are being unreasonable if

   a. you are unwilling to listen to someone's reasons.

   b. you are irritated by reasons people give you (before thinking them through).

   c. you become defensive during a discussion.

6. When you catch yourself being close-minded, analyze your thinking by completing the following statements in your journal (remember that the more details you write in your journal entries, the better able you will be to change your thinking in future similar situations):

   a. I realize I was being close-minded in this situation because...

   b. The thinking I was trying to hold onto is...

   c. Thinking that is potentially better is...

   d. This thinking is better because...

**"WE THINK SO BECAUSE OTHER PEOPLE THINK SO;
OR BECAUSE—OR BECAUSE—AFTER ALL,
WE DO THINK SO;
OR BECAUSE WE WERE TOLD SO,
AND THINK WE MUST THINK SO;
OR BECAUSE WE ONCE THOUGHT SO AND
THINK WE STILL THINK SO;
OR BECAUSE, HAVING THOUGHT SO,
WE THINK WE WILL THINK SO."
—HENRY SIDGWICK**

This is the day to *show mercy:*

Have Mercy

Have Mercy

Have Mercy

Be on the lookout for opportunities to show mercy to others, to display understanding, compassion, and forgiveness. Notice the extent to which others around you favor punishment and suffering as the proper response to "deviant" behavior. Notice the extent to which you do. As you read the newspaper, notice that severe sentences often are meted out for "crimes" that injure no one except the perpetrator.

Ask yourself how often punishment is extreme (in causing human suffering). Consider "three-strikes-and-you're-out" legislation. Consider the practice of trying children as adults. Consider "adult crime, adult time" legislation (laws aimed at giving adult-length sentences to children convicted of serious crimes). Also familiarize yourself with the approach of other countries (for example, Finland) that successfully return criminals to socially meaningful lives as soon as possible, with a low rate of repeat offenders. Think of ways to deal with cultural deviance without extreme punishment and social vengeance.

Day Thirteen:
Show Mercy

Most of us think that if other people were to think just like us, the world would be a better place. We naturally believe that what we think is right. And when people don't think like us and don't behave like us, we are often intolerant. We often want to see people punished for being different (though, of course, we wouldn't admit this). For example, more and more behaviors are being criminalized in the U.S. because of intolerance for others' lifestyles. Consider prostitution. Many people find it *disgusting* and *perverted*. They therefore want prostitutes punished (for their *repulsive* behavior). Similarly, many people are upset by the idea of recreational drug use. They see people who engage in recreational drugs as social menaces. They feel a sense of righteousness when drug users are locked up (even though they themselves might very well drink alcohol, smoke cigarettes, or use mind-altering prescription drugs). That there are now more people in jail in the U.S. per capita than in any other country in the world does not bother them. *Throw away the key* is their method! *Show no mercy*, their watchword! *Make them suffer*, their clarion call! Compassion, tolerance, and understanding are rare commodities. Though most people are compassionate toward their own family and close friends, few demonstrate compassion and tolerance toward those who think and act differently from themselves.

Strategies for showing compassion and mercy:

1. Whenever you think someone should be punished for his or her actions, stop and ask yourself whether the greater good might not be better served in some other way. For example, would it not be better, in many cases, to think rehabilitation rather than prison?

2. Whenever you think you are absolutely right and you judge another person's behavior to be intolerable, ask yourself: "What reasons do I have to support my view? How do I know I'm right? Could I be wrong? Am I being intolerant?"

3. Study the situations within which you find yourself most lacking in mercy, forgiveness, and understanding. In what situations do you think people should be punished rather than helped? On what reasoning do you base your conclusions?

4. Consider the influence of social conditioning on your ability to see things from multiple perspectives. To what extent does your culture encourage or discourage forgiveness and mercy? To what extent does your culture encourage revenge upon, and condemnation and punishment of, the "wicked?" To what extent have you uncritically accepted righteous and merciless views encouraged by your culture?

> **"WE HAND FOLKS OVER TO GOD'S MERCY,**
> **AND SHOW NONE OURSELVES."**
> **—GEORGE ELIOT**

This is the day to *think for yourself:*

Don't Conform

Don't Conform

Don't Conform

Assume that you are a conformist. Only when you can admit that you are a conformist can you begin to identify when and where you conform. Recognize that conformity occurs in virtually every domain of life. Look for it in the newspaper. Look for it in your relationships. Look for it in the groups to which you belong. Notice it at work. See it in others. Notice how people profess to be independent even when they are consummate conformists. Notice when you are most likely to conform. Notice when you are least likely to conform. Figure out the consequences of your conformity. Figure out the consequences of others' conformity. Think about political conformity. Think about the consequences of nationalism (as a form of mass conformity). Figure out when it makes sense to conform (for example, not talking loudly on your cell phone while in a restaurant) and when it doesn't (for example, mindlessly supporting unethical business or governmental practices).

Day Fourteen:
Don't Be a Conformist

Living a human life entails membership in a variety of human groups. This typically includes groups such as nation, culture, profession, religion, family, and peer group. We find ourselves participating in groups before we are aware of ourselves as living beings. We find ourselves in groups in virtually every setting in which we function as persons. What is more, every group to which we belong has some social definition of itself and unspoken "rules" that guide the behavior of all members. Each group to which we belong imposes some level of conformity on us as a condition of acceptance. This includes a set of beliefs, behaviors, requirements, and taboos.

All of us, to varying degrees, accept as right and correct whatever ways of acting and believing are fostered in the social groups to which we belong. Typically, this acceptance is uncritical.

Group membership clearly offers some advantages. But those advantages come with a price. Many people behave unethically because it is expected of them. Groups impose their rules (conventions, folkways, taboos) on individuals. Group membership is in various ways "required" for ordinary acts of living. Suppose, for example, that you wanted to legally belong to no nation, to be a citizen not of a country *but of the world.* You would not be allowed that freedom. You would find that you were allowed no place to live, nor any way to travel from place to place. Every place in the world is claimed by some nation (as its "sovereign" possession), and every nation requires that all visitors to it come as citizens of some other country (thus, with a "passport"). In addition, everywhere a nation imposes its "sovereignty," it requires the obedience of all persons to literally thousands (if not hundreds of thousands) of laws.

For most people, blind conformity to group restrictions is automatic and unreflective. Most people effortlessly conform without recognizing their conformity. They internalize group norms and beliefs, take on the group identity, and act as they are expected to act—without the least sense that what they are doing might reasonably be questioned. Most people function in social groups as unreflective participants in a range of beliefs, attitudes, and behaviors analogous to those of urban street gangs.

And conformity is one of the evils of human society. Why? Because through conformity, *arbitrary* social rules are treated as if they were *inherently* good and right. Arbitrary social rules lead to any number of unjust practices. Consider the ways in which people who do not abide by social conventions are marginalized within a culture. For example, consider the groups who tend to be marginalized in the U.S.—atheists, people who protest wars, people who speak out against unethical government practices when the mainstream is not speaking out. Furthermore, consider how arbitrary social conventions often lead to arbitrary laws, the enforcement of which often results in human suffering (for example, unjust prison sentences).

When you have developed as a skilled, independent thinker, you do not mindlessly follow the crowd. You think for yourself. You figure out for yourself what makes sense to believe and what to reject. You recognize social rules and taboos for what they often are: subjective creations of an unthinking mass.

Of course, it is often quite difficult to critically analyze the cultural conventions existing within one's own culture. These conventions are systematically indoctrinated into our thinking throughout a lifetime. As the reigning beliefs, they surround us. Overcoming indoctrination requires committed effort, insight, and courage.

Strategies for becoming an independent thinker:

1. Write down your answers to these questions: What are some of the taboos in my culture? What behaviors are considered *shocking* or *disgusting*? What beliefs are treated as sacred? What penalties exist for people who do not abide by social rules, even though their behavior doesn't hurt anyone (and even though these rules come and go over the years)?

2. Notice how cultural taboos and rules are fostered within the culture. Note, for example, how often messages about "good" and "bad" behavior are the focus of TV programs and movies. Consider, for example, the number of TV programs focused on the police "catching" people in possession of illegal drugs, on the "good guys" catching the "bad guys" and locking them up. Do you find yourself cheering on the "good guys" and hoping the "bad guys get what's coming to them?" If so, why? In the real world, more harm and suffering are often caused by the official "good guys" than the official "bad guys." See if you can identify some examples.

3. Examine the extent to which you uncritically accept the taboos and requirements of your culture and social groups. Monitor your conformity. Begin a list of ways in which you can begin to think independently.

4. Make a list of problems that people experience as a result of mass conformity to arbitrary social rules. How do you contribute to those problems?

5. Read W.G. Sumner's book *Folkways*,[5] in which he describes a broad range of societies and behaviors within varying time periods. Imagine yourself living within those various cultures. What beliefs would you hold dear? How would you behave? How would your beliefs and behaviors differ from your current beliefs and behaviors?

6. Notice the extent to which your friends and family members conform to whatever social ideology is reigning at the moment. Notice the extent to which you are stifled by the groups to which you belong (those groups you choose to belong to, and those you belong to because you have no choice). Realize that independent thinkers often prefer to be alone, rather than attempt to fit into groups that irrationally and mindlessly conform to arbitrary social rules. Recognize that there is one free community you can always join—the community of independent thinkers found in the best books that have ever been written. Independent thinkers can always find a range of great thinkers waiting for them at the library.

**"IT IS THE PROOF OF A BAD CAUSE WHEN IT IS
APPLAUDED BY THE MOB."
—SENECA**

---

[5] *Folkways*, by W.G. Sumner, Salem, NH, Ayer Company Publishers (1992; originally published in 1906).

This is the day to *abandon domination:*

Don't Dominate

Don't Dominate

Don't Dominate

Be on the lookout for dominating behavior—yours and others'. Notice when people use language to dominate and control others. Detect differences between what they say and what they mean. Study your behavior to determine when and whom you tend to dominate. Are you "successful?" Is it worth it? Do you know anyone who routinely dominates people? Of course, there are circumstances when it is essential for one person to be in control, and when that person does so *reasonably* (as with the captain of a ship or a parent supervising a young child). Top-dog behavior, on the other hand, is designed to exercise power over others to serve one's interest or get what one wants.

Day Fifteen:
Don't Be a Top Dog

Top-dog behavior involves an attempt to control others to your advantage (and their disadvantage) by dominating them. One of the problems in human life stems from the tendency of some to dominate others. It is obvious in those who bully. But domination is often indirect and therefore difficult to detect. Human domination through manipulation plays a central role in modern society. It is almost always harmful to the persons being thus controlled. Much human suffering results from this tendency in human behavior.

People who are successful at dominating others, people who can get others to do what they want through direct control, power, or manipulation, may be among those least likely to change. This is true because "successful" dominators tend to experience positive emotions. They usually see things as going well for them. They like their life and tend to think that their relationships are generally good (even when others in the relationship are unhappy). If you are one of these people, you will have to work harder to change (than someone who experiences the negative consequences of his or her controlling behavior). You will have to change, then, not because you experience emotional pain or obvious problems in relationship to others, but because you recognize the unethical nature of dominating behavior.

Rational persons do not want to dominate others, even when they can, even when they personally benefit from doing so. They would rather give up something themselves than hurt others to get what they want.

As you develop your rational capacity, you become less dominating and less subject to the domination of others.

Strategies for becoming less dominating:

1. Identify areas in your life in which you irrationally try to control others. At home? At work? With your spouse? Your partner? Your children?

2. Now consider the consequences. Are you really "successful" in getting what you want? To what extent does it lead to fulfillment? To what extent does it lead to frustration? Is it worth it?

3. Notice how people "justify" dominating others. Note the reasons they give. Probe the actual reasons. Observe the usual results of domination in different situations.

4. Legal, economic, and military domination are common in human history and are always seen by dominators as justified and essential. Develop your awareness of individuals and groups who invest energy and resources in controlling others. Notice how often "dominating" behavior is justified as "self-defense" or "in the interest of the person/group being dominated."

"HATEFUL IS THE POWER, AND PITIABLE IS THE LIFE, OF THOSE WHO WISH TO BE FEARED RATHER THAN TO BE LOVED."
—CORNELIUS NEPOS

This is the day to *be independent:*

Don't Be Subservient

Don't Be Subservient

B e on the lookout for submissive behavior—yours and others'. One of the hallmarks of submissiveness is conformity, a phenomenon common in human life. People who are submissive to others often feel resentment. Notice when you are resentful after having "gone along." When you submit against your will, do you notice yourself doing so, do you feel impotent, or do you just think negative thoughts? Perhaps you make a flippant or sarcastic comment. Perhaps you act in a passive/aggressive way. Don't blame others for controlling you when you do not take control of yourself. Also notice when others are submissive in relationship to you. Can you figure out what they are after? Do they get what they want through their submissive behavior?

Day Sixteen:
Don't Be an Underdog

A person playing an underdog role submits to the domination of another or others in exchange for security, protection, or advancement. These people exchange their freedom to achieve these ends (real or imagined). The underdog learns the art of helplessness. Characteristics typically include submissiveness, servility, or subservience, often accompanied by feelings of inferiority, inadequacy, and resentment. The underdog gains some indirect influence over the top dog through flattering subservience. Ironically, clever underdogs sometimes "control" unskillful top dogs. Underdogs can be either successful or unsuccessful in achieving their goals.

People are often subservient in some situations and dominating in others. In other words, they may switch roles in different situations. For example, they might be subservient at the office and dominating at home, or subservient to their spouse while dominating their children. At other times they may be rational.

Top-dog/underdog patterns are played out in numerous settings and situations in human life, and they lead to much suffering, injustice, and cruelty.

Rational persons avoid playing either of these roles. They recognize top-dog and underdog patterns in themselves, insofar as they exist, and they work to avoid them.

Note that going along with a decision when you disagree with it is not necessarily egocentric submissive (or underdog) behavior. For example, if another person knows more about a situation or issue than you do, and you are not in a position to research the information yourself, it might make sense to go along (even though the little information you have about the situation would lead you to disagree). You have to decide, in any given situation and at any given moment, whether you are egocentrically submitting to others or whether you are rationally conceding.

To get command of your subservient nature, to the extent that you are prone to this tendency, begin observing your behavior closely when you are with others. Do you tend to go along with others without thinking through whether it makes sense to do so? Do you resent doing so afterwards? Do you feel like someone else has control over you? Only by bringing your subservient thinking and behavior to the forefront of your thoughts will you be able to get command of it and change it.

Strategies for avoiding irrational submission:

1. Pinpoint underdog behavior in yourself by identifying situations in which you tend to go along with others without good reason to do so. In these situations you may very well resent the subservient role you play. Yet your resentment is submerged. You don't explicitly resist. You say what you are expected to say (but don't really mean). After going along, you blame others for your frustration. To what extent do you find yourself behaving in a subservient way in your everyday life? Why are you doing it? What are you getting for doing it? What do you think would happen if you spoke up and said what you really think? What do you think you would lose?

2. See if you can identify *specific circumstances* in the past in which you behaved in a submissive manner. Did you feel resentful? Defensive? Irritable? Intimidated?

3. Much submissiveness in society goes unnoticed. And most people are egocentrically submissive in some areas of their lives. For example, most people do not recognize their submission to their peer group, to irrational cultural requirements and taboos, or to socially-defined authorities (people with high social status) who may lead people to act against their interests. Ask yourself how important it is to be your own person, to think for yourself, and to be in command of your life. Insisting you are free does not make you free. Freedom begins with recognizing the extent of your slavery and subservience to social conventions, rules, and ideology.

4. Realize that the underdog, like the top dog, can be either successful or unsuccessful. To the extent that you egocentrically submit to others, how "successful" are you? Do you tend to get what you want through submission? What precisely are you getting? What price are you paying for the reward? To what extent are you being dishonest in the situation—either with yourself or others?

5. Try to catch yourself being submissive, such as in a meeting or in a conversation. At that moment, speak up. Say, as rationally as possible, precisely what you think. Notice the sense of self you gain.

6. Take a global look at your behavior to determine the extent to which you are dominating, submissive, or rational. In what areas of your life do you tend to dominate? In what areas do you tend to submit? In what areas are you rational? What percentage of the time are you dominating, submissive, or rational? Start observing yourself closely to take control of yourself. When you do, you may be surprised by the inner sense of integrity you gain.

**"NO MAN IS FREE WHO IS NOT MASTER OF HIMSELF."
—EPICTETUS**

This is the day to *stop worrying:*

Stop Worrying

Stop Worrying

Stop Worrying

B e on the lookout for when you worry about problems rather than taking action to solve them. Notice when you are worrying while presenting a calm, unruffled exterior. Notice the negative emotions you experience when you worry. Notice when others worry, fail to act (when they can), and instead waste energy in emoting about a problem. When you catch yourself worrying, apply the Mother Goose rhyme on the next page to the situation. Act to solve problems (when you can). Let them go if you can't.

Worrying never adds to the quality of your life, but it can certainly diminish its quality.

Day Seventeen:
Don't Be a Worrywart

Many people go through life worrying about problems rather than actively working to solve them. Sometimes they obsess about problems they can do nothing about. Consider the wisdom in this simple Mother Goose rhyme:

For every problem under the sun,
there is a solution or there is none.
If there be one, seek till you find it.
If there be none, then never mind it.

It is remarkable how seldom people follow this sage advice. When faced with a problem, you first need to do your best thinking to see if you can find a solution. Open your mind to alternative possibilities. If you determine that you cannot solve the problem, you need to let it go. Worrying and obsessing about something out of your control is emotionally painful and fruitless. Realize that, to the extent that you worry, instead of actively looking for solutions, your mind is failing you. Force your reflective mind into action. Identify the real options. Figure out the best one. Focus your energy on pursuing it. If there is nothing you can do in the situation, let it go; turn your mind to something productive.

Strategies for relinquishing the worrying habit:

1. For every problem you have difficulty handling, follow Mother Goose. Ask yourself:

   a. What precisely is the problem?

   b. What are my options? Is there a possible solution under my control? Have I exhausted all possibilities for a solution? Have I considered every option available to me?

   c. If this is a problem I cannot solve, or if I have exhausted all realistic options, am I letting go of the problem? Or am I still worrying about it? If so, why?

2. Make a list of all the problems you worry about. Then go through the preceding steps for each one.

3. Make a list of all the problems you have ever worried over and the results of those worries. To what extent did worrying help solve the problems? What were some consequences of your worrying? Which of those problems could you have solved through good thinking?

4. Be proactive whenever you can. When faced with a troubling situation, don't allow your energy to be sapped by fretful worrying and obsessing. Instead, take action whenever you can, and to whatever extent you can. Use your energy productively, rather than destructively.

5. Suppose you have done your best thinking about a problem but nevertheless have been unable to solve it. Notice your mind beginning to worry. At that point, immediately intervene with productive thinking. Remind yourself of Mother Goose. Rethink the situation. Dig up new relevant information you previously missed, if possible. Keep concentrated on action. Be a doer, not a worrywart.

"WORRY IS INTEREST PAID ON TROUBLE BEFORE IT BECOMES DUE."
—W.R. INGE

This is the day to *stop blaming your parents:*

Stop Blaming Your Parents

Stop Blaming Your Parents

Some people spend years of their lives blaming their parents for emotional problems they have had. They obsess about their parents' mistakes. Focus your energy today on letting go of the emotional "damage" you think your parents did to you. The past is gone. The present and future remain. Thinking negative thoughts about your parents doesn't help them—or you. Whenever you think negative thoughts about your parents, remind yourself that you now can create who you are becoming. Stop feeling sorry for yourself. Stop wallowing in the past. Begin living in the here and now. Start re-creating yourself. Only you stand in your way. Only *you* can leave the past in the past.

Day Eighteen:
Stop Blaming Your Parents

Very few people survive childhood without emotional scars. All parents make mistakes. Some make significant mistakes, leading to emotional scars for their children. But as adults, we need to take responsibility for who we are and who we are becoming. This involves recognizing emotional baggage and getting past it. Living in misery, blaming our parents, and focusing on ourselves as victims lead to a life of depression and resentment. We have a choice. By taking charge of our thinking (and thus our emotions and desires), we can become who we want to be. We can become the author of our life. We can leave emotional baggage behind.[6]

Strategies for taking charge of who you are:

1. If you really think you have something significant to blame your parents for, write down exactly what that is and what the damage was to your emotional well-being. Make sure you distinguish between *fact* and *belief.* Belief can produce a self-fulfilling prophecy. Believing you have been harmed can result in harm. For example, believing that your parents destroyed your chance to pursue higher education, you may fail to pursue it—to get revenge on them.

2. After you have compiled your list, read it carefully. Then ask yourself what you hope to gain by dwelling on any of these negative memories. Do you, as an adult, need to live in the past, as if you were still a child, unable to control your situation? Have you become a slave to unpleasant memories? Why not instead focus on what you can control, on opportunities, on what you can do?

3. Take every moment you typically use to feed negative emotions about your parents, and transform your energy into action that leads to potential success and therefore positive emotions. For

---

[6] We acknowledge that some emotional scars are so deep that you cannot solve them without professional help. We also realize that some people have been scarred so deeply that they perhaps never become emotionally healthy. We are focused here on the vast majority of problems over which a person does have control.

example, what can you learn from the mistakes your parents made? What can you do to be different, wiser, more just, more compassionate than your parents were?

4. Make a list of all the sacrifices your parents made for you, and all the many everyday things they did for you. Then ask yourself if you have given them sufficient credit for their good deeds. Many parents deserve far more credit than they get from their children, despite the mistakes they make.

5. When you visit your parents or talk to them on the phone, don't dwell on the past. If necessary, think of your parents as people you have just met. Try to take them as they are now. If your parents are still engaging in the behavior you perceive as harmful to you, perhaps you need to keep your distance from them. Perhaps you need to live away from them. Either way, act positively.

Consider the wisdom in this ancient Hawaiian proverb: "Either you eat life or life eats you." Only you—not your parents—can determine which of these two possibilities you embrace.

"NEVER DOES THE HUMAN SOUL APPEAR SO STRONG AND NOBLE AS WHEN IT FOREGOES REVENGE, AND DARES TO FORGIVE AN INJURY."
—E.H. CHAPIN

This is the day to *critique the news media:*

Critique the News Media

Critique the News Media

A ctively critique the *products* of the news media throughout the day. Study the newspaper carefully, noting how "friends" of one's country are presented positively while its "enemies" are presented negatively. Notice the not-so-important articles on the front page versus the important articles buried within. Notice significant world problems being ignored or played down while the sensational is highlighted. Imagine how you would rewrite news stories to broaden their perspectives or to present issues more fairly. Make critical reading of the news a habit, not a rare event. Notice how TV news programs oversimplify the complex. Note how they target whatever they can sensationalize, and how they tend to dwell on stories that will be considered sensational by their viewers (rather than focusing on what is significant or deep). Note how they create and feed social hysteria.

Day Nineteen: Don't Be Brainwashed by the News Media

Each society and culture has a unique worldview. This worldview shapes what people see and how they see it. It shapes perceptions and beliefs. News media across the world reflect the worldview of their own culture. This is true both because those who work in national news media share the same views as their readers and because they need to *sell* what people within the culture want to *buy*. They need to present the news in ways that are palatable and interesting to their audience so as to increase their profits. In the book *The News About the News*, Downie and Kaiser present the problems as follows:

> *"The national television networks have trimmed their reporting staffs and closed foreign reporting bureaus to cut their owners' costs. They have tried to attract viewers by diluting their expensive newscasts with lifestyle, celebrity, and entertainment features, and by filling their low-budget, high-profit, prime time 'newsmagazines' with sensational sex, crime, and court stories"* (New York: Knopf, 2002), p.19.

Mainstream news coverage in any culture operates on the following (often unconscious) maxims:

- "This is how it appears to us from our point of view; therefore, this is the way it is."
- "These are the facts that support our way of looking at this; therefore, these are the most important facts."
- "These countries are friendly to us; therefore, these countries deserve praise."
- "These countries are unfriendly to us; therefore, these countries deserve criticism."
- "These are the stories most interesting or sensational to our readers; therefore, these are the most important stories in the news."

But the truth of what is happening in the world is far more complicated than what appears true to people in any culture.

If you do not recognize bias in your nation's news; if you cannot detect ideology, slant, and spin; if you cannot recognize propaganda when exposed to it, you cannot reasonably determine what media messages have to be supplemented, counterbalanced, or thrown out entirely. These insights are crucial to becoming a critical consumer of the news media and developing skills of media analysis.

Strategies for seeing through the news media:

1. Study alternative perspectives and worldviews, learning how to interpret events from the perspective of multiple views.
2. Seek understanding and insight through multiple sources of thought and information, not simply those of the mass media.
3. Learn how to identify the viewpoints embedded in news stories.
4. Mentally rewrite (reconstruct) news stories through awareness of how they would be told from multiple perspectives.
5. See news stories as one way of representing reality (as some blend of fact and interpretation).
6. Assess news stories for their clarity, accuracy, relevance, depth, breadth, and significance.
7. Notice contradictions and inconsistencies in the news (often in the same story).
8. Notice the agenda and interests a story serves.
9. Notice the facts covered and the facts ignored.
10. Notice what is represented as fact that should be presented as debatable.
11. Notice assumptions implicit in stories.
12. Notice what is implied but not openly stated.
13. Notice what implications are ignored and what are highlighted.
14. Notice which points of view are systematically presented favorably and which are presented unfavorably.

15. Mentally correct stories that reflect bias toward the unusual, the dramatic, and the sensational by putting them into perspective or discounting them.

16. Notice when social conventions and taboos are used to define issues and problems as unethical.

"ALL JOURNALISTS ARE, BY VIRTUE OF THEIR HANDICRAFT, ALARMISTS; THIS IS THEIR WAY OF MAKING THEMSELVES INTERESTING."
–LORD RIDDELL

This is the day to *notice the vested interest of politicians:*

See Through Politicians

Empathize with Others
Uncover Your Ignorance
Notice Contradictions
Be Fair, Not Selfish
Stick to Your Purpose
Be Clear
Be Relevant
Question, Question, Question
Think Through Implications
Control Your Emotions
Control Your Desires
Be Reasonable
Show Mercy
Think for Yourself
Don't Be a Top Dog
Don't Be an Underdog
Don't Be a Worrywart
Stop Blaming Your Parents
Critique the News Media
See Through Politicians
Be a Citizen of the World
Notice Media Garbage
Make Your Mark
Educate Yourself
Figure Out Where to Go

See Through Politicians

A s you go through your day, think about distinguishing politicians from statesmen. Politicians are people who pursue power to advance their vested interests. Statesmen are people who genuinely seek what is in the public interest. They are willing to state unpopular views and stand up against powerful groups and vested interests.

Be on the lookout for questionable statements that politicians make. Look on the surface at what they say. Look beneath the surface at what they mean. Determine what is in their vested interest. Notice how often their behavior supports their own interest while appearing to serve the good of the people or country. Figure out what they want you to believe and why. Notice how they oversimplify problems to manipulate people. Notice how they often assert "truths" that contradict reality (which they blatantly ignore). Notice how often people believe them nevertheless.

Day Twenty:
Don't Be Bamboozled by Politicians

Politicians would have us believe that they are deeply concerned about the welfare of the people, that their actions are determined by what best serves the people. In other words, politicians present themselves as statesmen. Don't buy it. President Lyndon Johnson said, "Money is the mother's milk of politics." If you read between the lines, you will see quite easily that in politics, money, not concern for the public interest, is usually where the action is, with big money protecting big money. Consider this example from the news:[7]

> *"The Bush administration announced Thursday it will demand significant changes to a major World Health Organization initiative to battle obesity, saying the plan is based on faulty scientific evidence and exceeds the U.N. body's mandate.... The WHO plan, which outlines strategies nations can use to fight obesity, has been widely applauded by public health advocates but bitterly opposed by some food manufacturers and the sugar industry."*

Needless to say, food manufacturers and the sugar industry have a vested interest in avoiding the obesity issue, since they are primary contributors to it. In many cases such as this, big business rules politics even at the expense of public health. Of course, this is one of many examples of money driving political decisions. If politicians don't do what those who bankroll them want, their money supply is cut off. Their primary concern is getting re-elected. In politics, sound bites, catchphrases, glitzy images, and mass delivery are the mechanisms for manipulating the people. Of course, there are a few needles in the haystack—someone running for election who is not bought and paid for by big money. But such a person usually doesn't get elected.

Critical thinkers are not manipulated by slick-talking politicians. They recognize how politics works. Examine your thinking about politicians. How gullible are you when it comes to believing what politicians say? How often do you compare what they say with what they do?

---

[7] "White House to Demand WHO Obesity Plan Changes," The Santa Rosa, Calif. *Press Democrat*, Jan. 16, 2004.

Strategies for seeing through politicians:

1. Listen closely to what politicians say, identifying how they manipulate the electorate (for example, by using language that reinforces stereotypes or provokes unnecessary fear). Always ask, "What is the interest of big money here?" And, conversely, "What is in the public interest?" Note the dearth of politicians acting in the public interest.

2. Notice how politicians usually reflect dominant belief systems and reigning ideologies within the culture. That is, note how they lack intellectual autonomy.

3. Keep in mind the vested interest of politicians. This will enable you to predict their behavior.

4. Become a student of political history, reading broadly in alternative sources to identify repeating patterns in political behavior throughout the years. Which of these patterns are prevalent today?

5. Notice the extent to which politicians are entrenched in superficial and simplistic views. Nuances and depth cannot be expressed in sound bites.

**"TO BE A CHEMIST YOU MUST STUDY CHEMISTRY;
TO BE A LAWYER OR PHYSICIAN YOU MUST STUDY LAW
OR MEDICINE; BUT TO BE A POLITICIAN YOU NEED ONLY TO
STUDY YOUR OWN INTERESTS."
—MAX O'RELL**

This is the day to *be a citizen of the world:*

Be a Citizen of the World

Be a Citizen of the World

It is becoming increasingly clear that the survival and well-being of humans depends largely on our ability to work together successfully and productively, to reach out to one another, to help one another. Yet, problems of nationalism and ethnocentrism are pervasive across the world. People are raised to see their country, or their group, as better than other countries or groups. They tend to favor the groups to which they belong. This is a natural tendency of the human mind. And it is a tendency fostered within most, if not all, cultures. By doing just a little research (for example, reading the newspaper, watching the news, reading traditional history books about your country), you can easily notice how often people present their country as the best country in the world. Notice how they whitewash their country's motives, representing them in glowing ethical terms (We are just! We are fair! We are good!). Notice how the national press fosters this image. Think of what you were taught in school about your country. Think about which parts of your country's history were ignored or distorted. Think about how your government describes its foreign policies (professing to care about other countries while its true motive is often to maintain a certain image or pursue some selfish goal).

Day Twenty-One:
Strive to Be a Citizen of the World

In most countries, people are socialized to think in terms that advance the interests of their country—to be, in a word, *nationalists*: "We are the best. We are number one. We stand for justice, truth, and freedom. When countries disagree with us, they are wrong. If they actively oppose us, they are our enemies. We sometimes make mistakes, but we always mean well. Those who oppose us usually have irrational, or even evil, motives. They are jealous of us." This pathological way of thinking, when centered in a culture, is called ethnocentrism. It is universal. And it is decidedly destructive.

In his book *Folkways*,[8] W.G. Sumner puts the problem of ethnocentricity as follows:

> *"Every group of any kind whatsoever demands that each of its members shall help defend group interests. The group force is also employed to enforce the obligations of devotion to group interests. It follows that judgments are precluded and criticism silenced.... The patriotic bias is a recognized perversion of thought and judgment against which our education should guard us"* (p. 15).

If we are to create a world that advances justice for the vast majority of people across the globe, we must become *citizens of the world*. We must denounce nationalism[9] and ethnocentrism. We must think within a global, rather than national, view. We must take a long-term view. We must begin to relegate the interests of any given country, including our own, to that of one of many: no more worthy, no more needy, no more deserving of the world's resources than anyone else on the planet. We must see the lives of people in other countries as no less precious than the lives of people in our own country. We must oppose the pursuit of narrow selfish or group interests. Integrity and justice must become more important to us than national advantage and power.

---

[8]   *Folkways*, by W.G. Sumner, Salem, N.H., Ayer Company Publishers (1992) (originally published in 1906).

[9]   Defined by *Webster's New World Dictionary* as militant, unreasoning, and boastful devotion to one's country or culture; excessive, narrow, or jingoist patriotism.

Strategies for becoming a citizen of the world:

1. Question the motives and actions of all governments. Recognize the similarity of politicians in all countries. Recognize the similarity of news media—serving vested interests—in all countries. Do not be taken in by emotional appeals. Base your decisions on universal values, not on national interests. Support the development of altruistic international groups unconnected to vested interests.

2. Imagine yourself a *citizen of the world.* Put world needs ahead of national agendas. Study problems from a global and historical point of view. Notice how the world and countries are stratified—with the "rules of the game" favoring the few, the powerful, and the wealthy.

3. Notice the evolution of your views as you learn to think within a global perspective.

4. Take one world problem—for instance, global warming, malnutrition, disease, overpopulation—and find out as much as you can from multiple international sources. Then compare what your nation is doing about the problem. Are you surprised by what you find?

"IF PATRIOTISM IS 'THE LAST REFUGE OF A SCOUNDREL,' IT IS NOT MERELY BECAUSE EVIL DEEDS MAY BE PERFORMED IN THE NAME OF PATRIOTISM...BUT BECAUSE PATRIOTIC FERVOR CAN OBLITERATE MORAL DISTINCTIONS ALTOGETHER."
—RALPH BARTON PERRY

This is the day to *critique T V, movies, and ads:*

Critique TV Shows
Critique Movies
Critique Ads

Empathize with Others
Uncover Your Ignorance
Notice Contradictions
Be Fair, Not Selfish
Stick to Your Purpose
Be Clear
Be Relevant
Question, Question, Question
Think Through Implications
Control Your Emotions
Control Your Desires
Be Reasonable
Show Mercy
Think for Yourself
Don't Be a Top Dog
Don't Be an Underdog
Don't Be a Worrywart
Stop Blaming Your Parents
Critique the News Media
See Through Politicians
Be a Citizen of the World
Notice Media Garbage
Make Your Mark
Educate Yourself
Figure Out Where to Go

Carefully observe your TV and movie-watching habits today. Note how much time you spend watching TV. Realize that most TV programs are aimed at the intellectual level of an eleven-year-old. Ask yourself what you might accomplish if you spent less time in front of the TV. Ask yourself what you are getting in return for the time you spend watching TV. Notice the types of programs you tend to select. Think through the implications of what you watch. What "messages" are you routinely receiving? Begin to notice the nationalistic or ethnocentric messages you see on TV. What cultural norms are being encouraged? What taboos are being discouraged? What types of behavior are sensationalized? How many programs include some form of violence? How many of those types of programs do you tend to watch? Also, pay close attention to the advertisements you see on TV. How are products being pitched to you, the potential buyer? Think about what advertisers assume about buyers. Pledge not to buy anything you see advertised today unless you independently assess the purchase in advance. Identify and begin to read at least one article or book on how ads influence people.

Day Twenty-Two:
Don't Get Your Views from
TV, Ads, and Movies

Group norms are propagated through virtually every structure in society, including mainstream television and movies, as well as advertising. Most of what is on TV is superficial. Most TV shows aim to engage and amuse, not to challenge the mind or to educate. Every day we are bombarded with messages that insult our intelligence while seeking to manipulate or influence our psyche (through intentional, subliminal messages). The vast majority of TV programs, movies, and ads attract us either by feeding simplistic emotional beliefs (which flatter our infantile mind), or by stimulating our primitive drives for sexual gratification and violent revenge, or both. And it is merely naiveté or self-deception to say that you are not influenced by the shows you watch.

Strategies for critiquing TV shows, ads, and movies:

1. Notice the TV shows that focus on violence: the violence of the "bad guys" in harming "good guys" and the violence of the "good guys" in taking violent revenge on the "bad guys" for their violence (you get to watch it both ways). What do you think are some consequences of TV violence?

2. Notice how rarely the mass media portray reasonable people doing reasonable things to advance a more reasonable world. For example, notice how often irrational behavior in "intimate" relationships is portrayed as perfectly normal and natural (I hate you and I love you! I hate you because I love you! If you don't love me, I'll kill you!).

3. Seek alternative TV channels that question the status quo, such as Free Speech TV and C-SPAN.

4. Log the time you spend watching TV. How could you spend your time more productively? Are you reading books that develop your mind? Are you reading anything that questions the status quo?

5. Carefully choose the movies you watch. Consider watching realistic and insightful independently produced or foreign movies, rather than superficial Hollywood movies.

6. Monitor your buying habits. How often do you buy the "advertised" brand? What does this tell you about yourself?

7. Note the use of sexually suggestive images in product advertisements. Ask yourself: Will I really be more sexy if I buy and use this product?

8. Rent the movie *Supersize Me*. Compare the information you get about McDonald's food in the movie with the information provided in the multitude of McDonald's ads. Think critically about food advertisements you see on TV. Compare the information these ads give you with the information they leave out (about what is in the food, about the health consequences of eating the food, and so on).

"WHY SHOULD PEOPLE GO OUT AND PAY TO SEE BAD
FILMS WHEN THEY CAN STAY AT HOME AND SEE BAD
TELEVISION FOR NOTHING?"
—SAMUEL GOLDWYN

This is the day to *contribute something to the world:*

Contribute

Contribute

Contribute

B e on the lookout for opportunities to improve the quality of life on Earth. Make a list of all the things you do currently to contribute to others' lives, or to the health of the Earth. Notice what others around you do. Do those around you contribute to a more just world, or do they mainly serve themselves? Make a list of some additional things you can do. Think about how you can fit into your schedule or your life some new ways of contributing. If you don't have a lot of time to spare, think about making greater financial contributions. But do something.

Day Twenty-Three:
Do Something, Anything,
to Help Make the World Better

You need only to look around you to see problems in the world, problems caused largely by humans. The goal of critical thought is to improve how we think and how we act both in our personal lives and in relationship to others. As such, insofar as you are a critical thinker, you want to improve the quality of life on Earth. When you think critically, there are implications for how you treat and relate to others. You can contribute to a more just and sane world in many ways. From an ethical point of view, each of us is obligated to help others who are incapable of helping themselves. Each of us is ethically charged with doing *what we can* to improve the quality of life, both of humans and of other creatures susceptible to pain and suffering.

Strategies for contributing to a more just world:

1. Carefully select a group that is organized to contribute to a better world. Many groups are fighting for justice in the world, for improved conditions, for the alleviation of pain and suffering. Select from local, national, and international groups. Select one and get involved—even if this means only sending money.

2. Think about your circle of influence and act, using that influence to help others. For example, can you improve the quality of life for the people you work with? What about the people you live with? Work to create environments, wherever you can, where people help people. Notice how much you give to others and how much you take or demand for yourself.

3. Discover your strengths, and use those strengths to contribute in any way that you can. If you are good at writing, you might write letters to newspaper editors. If you have other special talents, use them to contribute to a better world. Everything, however little, counts.

4. Most important of all, read widely and critically well-researched books on a range of world problems. You may be surprised to see how many world problems exist precisely because greed, selfishness, and vested interests dominate world resources.

"YOU WILL FIND THAT THE MERE RESOLVE NOT TO BE USELESS, AND THE HONEST DESIRE TO HELP OTHER PEOPLE, WILL, IN THE QUICKEST AND DELICATEST WAYS, IMPROVE YOURSELF."
—RUSKIN

This is the day to *begin to educate yourself:*

Empathize with Others
Uncover Your Ignorance
Notice Contradictions
Be Fair, Not Selfish
Stick to Your Purpose
Be Clear
Be Relevant
Question, Question, Question
Think Through Implications
Control Your Emotions
Control Your Desires
Be Reasonable
Show Mercy
Think for Yourself
Don't Be a Top Dog
Don't Be an Underdog
Don't Be a Worrywart
Stop Blaming Your Parents
Critique the News Media
See Through Politicians
Be a Citizen of the World
Notice Media Garbage
Make Your Mark
Educate Yourself
Figure Out Where to Go

Educate Yourself

Educate Yourself

Educate Yourself

P lace the cultivation of your mind at the heart of your personal values. Begin to develop a plan for lifelong self-development. Study your own behavior. Lay bare contradictions and inconsistencies. Study the behavior of others. Notice how often ignorance is broadcast as knowledge. Notice how often what is arbitrary is presented as universal. See through to the shallowness of celebrity and status. See through pomp and ceremony. Vow to learn something important every day through reading. Recognize that deep learning of new ideas, continually integrated with ideas already internalized, is the key to the educated mind, and the key to living a rational life. Reflect on ideas of significance. Identify opportunities to be with people who are seeking to improve their minds. Create a library. Include in it works by the world's best thinkers past and present (including dissenting thinkers). Make it your home.

Day Twenty-Four:
Educate Yourself

Although many people complete many years of school, including undergraduate and graduate studies, few people are *truly educated*. Why? Because few people have learned *how* to learn meaningful ideas. They are not learners for life. Instead, they form a belief system and then defend it for the rest of their lives. There is little development in their views. They do not expand the horizons of their minds. To the extent that they do develop, they tend to do so in certain narrow or technical ways (such as learning skills for succeeding on the job, or learning skills needed for a hobby). They lack the intellectual skills and traits unique to an educated person.

In 1852, John Henry Newman gave a series of lectures on education, which were later compiled and published in the book *The Idea of a University*.[10] In it, he describes the impact that a well-designed education has on the mind of the learner:

> *"...the intellect, which has been disciplined to the perfection of its powers, which knows and thinks while it knows, which has learned to leaven the dense mass of facts and events with the elastic force of reason, such an intellect cannot be partial, cannot be exclusive, cannot be impetuous, cannot be at a loss, cannot but be patient, collected, and majestically calm, because it discerns the end in every beginning, the origin in every end...because it ever knows where it stands, and how its path lies from one point to another"* (p. 138).

In this book, we have introduced a number of the skills and traits of the educated mind. But what we have laid out is an array of places *to begin*. To learn at a deep level, you need to take an active approach to your learning, realizing that education occurs throughout your lifetime, not just during your school years, and then only through committed practice. You need to understand the process of lifelong learning and explicitly choose to engage in it.

---

[10] Newman, J. 1912. New York: Longman's, Green and Co.

Strategies for self-education:

1. **Read widely.** Read something every day that opens your mind to new and important ideas. Focus especially on great literature and the works of great thinkers. Go beyond current-day writings. Read the ideas of great dissenters throughout history. For suggested readings, see the section near the end of this book titled "Reading Backwards."

2. **Become your own historian, sociologist, and economist.** You cannot be educated without a broad historical, sociological, and economic perspective. Understanding what is really happening in the world requires studying human behavior over time, examining patterns and their implications. It means reading alternative historical accounts that help offset the ethnocentric accounts that dominate the worldview of most people the world over. It involves becoming aware of the arbitrary nature of (most) social norms and taboos. It requires distinguishing universal ethical principles from variable social rules and taboos. By gaining a broadly grounded worldview, you will be better able to critique international news and irrational social practices. You will increasingly become your own person.

3. **Acquire the principles of critical thinking,** tools at the heart of intellectual discipline and development. For additional resources, visit the Foundation for Critical Thinking (www.criticalthinking.org).

**"A HUMAN BEING IS NOT, IN ANY PROPER SENSE,
A HUMAN BEING TILL HE IS EDUCATED."
—H. MANN**

This is the day to *develop a plan:*

Where to Go
Where to Go
Where to Go

Empathize with Others
Uncover Your Ignorance
Notice Contradictions
Be Fair, Not Selfish
Stick to Your Purpose
Be Clear
Be Relevant
Question, Question, Question
Think Through Implications
Control Your Emotions
Control Your Desires
Be Reasonable
Show Mercy
Think for Yourself
Don't Be a Top Dog
Don't Be an Underdog
Don't Be a Worrywart
Stop Blaming Your Parents
Critique the News Media
See Through Politicians
Be a Citizen of the World
Notice Media Garbage
Make Your Mark
Educate Yourself
Figure Out Where to Go

Focus your energy today on designing the next phase of your self-development plan. Make a list of books you plan to read in the next few months. Figure out how you will continue to develop your critical thinking abilities from this point forward. Consider keeping a daily journal. Seek and regularly read alternative sources of news and world views.

Remember our early suggestion. Namely, after you work through the *25-day plan*, graduate yourself to a *25-week plan*, focusing on one idea per week, rather than one idea per day. If you do this, you will deepen your understanding of each idea. Every important idea has many connections to other important ideas. Powerful ideas are powerful in light of the important connections they have. Every week you will shift your emphasis. Your insights will multiply.

The worst plan is no plan. It is an approach that leads to low-level functioning. Remember, the pressure to conform to mass views continues unabated all your life. Your plan to become your own person should be driving you forward. Begin afresh each day. Every day is a chance for a new beginning. You, and you alone, are the key to your intellectual growth. Don't allow anything—or anyone—to deter you from this goal.

Day Twenty-Five:
Figure Out Where to Go from Here

You have now been introduced to twenty-four simple but powerful ideas. If you are to continue to develop, however, you should decide where you will go from here. Many strategies can help improve the quality of your life. One thing is certain: If you don't take a next step, there will be no next step. Like a rubber band that has been stretched, you will return to your original habits, into patterns of action based on beliefs you have unconsciously absorbed but did not mindfully select.

Remember that the mind is free only to the extent that it is in command of itself. In other words, your mind controls you—your thoughts, your emotions, your desires, your behavior. But do you control your mind? When you take command of your mind, you decide, using skills of rational thought, what ideas to accept and what to reject, what ideas to take seriously and what to ignore. You recognize the mind's natural desire toward selfishness, and you intervene with fair-minded thinking and behavior. You recognize the mind's natural tendency to be rigid and close-minded. You therefore intervene to open your mind to other ways of looking at things. You recognize the mind's natural tendency to go along with group ideology, and so you closely examine your own behavior in groups to identify when and where you tend to mindlessly conform.

You will be in command of your mind only to the extent that you develop and continually redevelop plans for further growth. Otherwise, the egocentric and sociocentric tendencies of your mind (as with all of us) will pull you back to your comfort zone. They will keep you trapped in the ideology and mental habits you have developed unconsciously, in ideas that need questioning. But the only way you will be able to *accurately assess* the ideas that guide your behavior is through intellectual discipline and skills you develop in your mind through your mind, consciously and deliberately.

So develop your plan for moving forward. Develop it today; revisit it every day.

Strategies for taking the next steps toward development:

1. Explore other critical thinking resources, including those in the book *Critical Thinking: Tools for Taking Charge of Your Professional and Personal Life*,[11] as well as the *Thinker's Guide Library*. (Visit www.criticalthinking.org to read about these guides, as well as other books and materials.)

2. Commit yourself to learning and applying one new and important idea every day (or every week).

3. Continue to explore the ideas in this book, keeping a log of your reflections.

4. Set aside a certain time each day for self-development. Make sure it is a time of peace and quiet. Realize that if you aren't willing to designate time for your mind to grow, you aren't really committed to your personal development.

"THE CHIEF ART OF LEARNING, AS LOCKE HAS OBSERVED,
IS TO ATTEMPT BUT LITTLE AT A TIME."
—JOHNSON

---

[11] Paul, R., and L. Elder. 2002. *Critical Thinking: Tools for Taking Charge of Your Professional and Personal Life*, Upper Saddle River: Pearson Education.

Reading Backwards

One of the most powerful ways to educate yourself, to open your mind to alternative ways of experiencing the world, and thus to counteract the influence of social conditioning and the mass media, is to *read backwards*—to read books printed 10 years ago, 20 years ago, 50 years ago, 100 years ago, 200 years ago, 500 years ago, 1,000 years ago, even 2,000 years ago and more. When you do so, you can step outside the presuppositions and ideologies of the present day and develop an informed world perspective.

When you read only in the present, no matter how extensively, you are apt to absorb widely shared misconceptions taught and believed today as the truth. The following is a sampling of authors whose writings will enable you to rethink the present, to reshape and expand your worldview:[12]

- **More than 2,000 years ago:** Plato, Aristotle, Aeschylus, Aristophanes
- **1200s:** Thomas Aquinas, Dante
- **1300s:** Boccaccio, Chaucer
- **1400s:** Erasmus, Francis Bacon
- **1500s:** Machiavelli, Cellini, Cervantès, Montaigne
- **1600s:** John Milton, Pascal, John Dryden, John Locke, Joseph Addison
- **1700s:** Thomas Paine, Thomas Jefferson, Adam Smith, Benjamin Franklin, Alexander Pope, Edmund Burke, Edward Gibbon, Samuel Johnson, Daniel Defoe, Goethe, Rousseau, William Blake
- **1800s:** Jane Austen, Charles Dickens, Emile Zola, Balzac, Dostoyevsky, Sigmund Freud, Karl Marx, Charles Darwin, John Henry Newman, Leo Tolstoy, the Brontes, Frank Norris, Thomas Hardy, Emile Durkheim, Edmond Rostand, Oscar Wilde
- **1900s:** Ambrose Bierce, Gustavus Myers, H.L. Mencken, William Graham Sumner, W.H. Auden, Bertolt Brecht, Joseph Conrad, Max Weber, Aldous Huxley, Franz Kafka, Sinclair Lewis, Henry James, George Bernard Shaw, Jean-Paul Sartre, Virginia Woolf, William Appleman Williams, Arnold Toynbee, C. Wright Mills, Albert Camus, Willa Cather, Bertrand Russell, Karl Mannheim,

---

[12] We recognize that this list of authors represents a decidedly Western worldview. We therefore recommend, once you have grounded yourself in deeply insightful authors from the Western world, that you then read works by the great Eastern authors. Contact us for a reading list of insightful Eastern authors.

Thomas Mann, Albert Einstein, Simone De Beauvoir, Winston Churchill, William J. Lederer, Vance Packard, Eric Hoffer, Erving Goffman, Philip Agee, John Steinbeck, Ludwig Wittgenstein, William Faulkner, Talcott Parsons, Jean Piaget, Lester Thurow, Robert Reich, Robert Heilbroner, Noam Chomsky, Jacques Barzun, Ralph Nader, Margaret Mead, Bronislaw Malinowski, Karl Popper, Robert Merton, Peter Berger, Milton Friedman, J. Bronowski

When you read backwards, you will come to understand some of the stereotypes and misconceptions of the present. You will develop a better sense of what is universal and what is relative, what is essential and what is arbitrary.

"IF WE ENCOUNTERED A MAN OF RARE INTELLIGENCE WE SHOULD ASK HIM WHAT BOOKS HE READ."
—RALPH WALDO EMERSON

Daily Action Plan

The key idea I am focused on today is:

The settings in which I can best practice using this idea are:

I plan to practice using this idea in the following ways (using the following strategies):

Daily Progress Notes

(To be completed at the end of each day)

Today I was successful in using the following ideas/strategies:

The key insights that emerged for me as I attempted to take ownership of this idea were:

One problem in my thinking that I now realize I need to work on is:

I plan to continue working on this problem in my thinking by using the following strategy:

Weekly Action Plan

The key idea for this week is:

The settings in which I can best practice using this idea are:

I plan to practice using this idea in the following ways (using these strategies):

Weekly Progress Notes

(To be completed at the end of each week)

This week I was successful in using the following ideas/strategies:

The key insights that emerged for me as I attempted to take ownership of this idea were:

One problem in my thinking that I now realize I need to work on is:

I plan to continue working on this problem in my thinking by using the following strategy:

Recommended Readings to Augment the Strategies

All of the following readings come from two sources—either passages from the book *Critical Thinking: Tools for Taking Charge of Your Professional and Personal Life* (CT), or volumes of the *Thinker's Guide Library* (TGL), both of which can be found at the Foundation for Critical Thinking (www.criticalthinking.org).

- Day One: Learn to Empathize with Others: CT pp. 26–27, 35. TGL: *Ethical Reasoning.*
- Day Two: Develop Knowledge of Your Ignorance: CT pp. 22–23, 33–34, 325.
- Day Three: Beware of Hypocrisy and Notice Contradictions in Your Life: CT pp. 27–28, 166.
- Day Four: Be Fair, Not Selfish: CT pp. 157–183. TGL: *The Human Mind.*
- Day Five: Know Your Purpose: CT pp. 76–78. TGL: *Analytic Thinking.*
- Day Six: Clarify Your Thinking: CT pp. 99–100.
- Day Seven: Stick to the Point: CT p. 103.
- Day Eight: Question, Question, Question: CT pp. 84–85. TGL: *Asking Essential Questions.*
- Day Nine: Think Through Implications: CT pp. 91–93, 126, 240, 322–323. TGL: *Analytic Thinking.*
- Day Ten: Get Control of Your Emotions: CT pp. 318–319. TGL: *The Human Mind.*
- Day Eleven: Take Control of Your Desires: CT pp. 40–45, 280. TGL: *The Human Mind.*
- Day Twelve: Be Reasonable: CT pp. 17–35, 183, 293–310.
- Day Thirteen: Show Mercy: CT pp. 22–23. TGL: *Ethical Reasoning.*
- Day Fourteen: Don't Be a Conformist: CT pp. 33, 185–203, 307.
- Day Fifteen: Don't Be a Top Dog: CT pp. 171–176, 305. TGL: *The Human Mind.*

- Day Sixteen: Don't Be an Underdog: CT pp. 171–176, 305. TGL: *The Human Mind*.
- Day Seventeen: Don't Be a Worrywart: CT pp. 146–151.
- Day Eighteen: Stop Blaming Your Parents: CT pp. 151–156.
- Day Nineteen: Don't Be Brainwashed by the News Media: CT pp. 134–135, 195–201. TGL: *How to Detect Media Bias and Propaganda*.
- Day Twenty: Don't Be Bamboozled by Politicians: CT pp. 232–236, 255–262.
- Day Twenty-One: Strive to Be a Citizen of the World: CT pp. 1–5, 201–202.
- Day Twenty-Two: Don't Get Your Views from TV, Ads, and Movies: CT pp. 134–135.
- Day Twenty-Three: Do Something, Anything, to Help Make the World Better: TGL: *Ethical Reasoning*.
- Day Twenty-Four: Educate Yourself: Visit www.criticalthinking.org for resources.
- Day Twenty-Five: Figure Out Where to Go from Here: CT pp. 47–57.
- Additional Strategies for Self-Development: CT pp. 277–310.

Index

The Thinkers Guide Library

The Thinkers Guide Library provides convenient, inexpensive, portable references you can use to improve the quality of your thinking—and therefore the quality of your life. Each guide focuses on one or more key concepts in critical thinking and/or applies critical thinking concepts to a specific domain of thought. Their succinctness serves as a continual reminder of the most basic principles of critical thinking. These guides are available through the Foundation for Critical Thinking at www. criticalthinking.org (800.833.3645).

The Miniature Guide to Critical Thinking Concepts and Tools—Contains the essence of critical thinking concepts and tools distilled into pocket size. These concepts can and should be applied to any and all domains of human life.

The Thinkers Guide to Analytic Thinking: How to Take Thinking Apart and What to Look for When You Do—Focuses on the intellectual skills that enable you to analyze anything you might think about—questions, problems, issues, fields of study, and more. It provides the common denominator between all forms of analysis.

The Thinkers Guide to How to Detect Media Bias and Propaganda in National and World News—Helps you recognize bias in your nation's news, to detect ideology, slant, and spin at work, and to recognize propaganda so that you can reasonably determine what media messages need to be supplemented, counter-balanced, or thrown out entirely. It focuses on the internal logic of the news as well as societal influences on the media.

The Thinkers Guide to Fallacies: The Art of Mental Trickery and Manipulation—Introduces you to the concept of fallacies in thinking and emphasizes the pervasive role that fallacies play in human life. It focuses on insights you need to protect yourself in a world where deception, duplicity, sophistry, delusion, and hypocrisy are the norm. It distinguishes between uncritical persons, skilled manipulators, and fair-minded critical persons and it introduces 44 foul ways that skilled, but self-serving thinkers, use to win arguments and manipulate people.

The Human Mind—Focuses on the basic functions of the human mind and how knowledge of these functions (and their interrelations) can enable you to use your intellect and emotions more effectively. Also introduces the problem of egocentricity as a primary barrier to the development of rational thought.

Understanding the Foundations of Ethical Reasoning—Provides insights into the nature of ethical reasoning, why it is so often flawed, and how to avoid those flaws. It lays out the function of ethics, its main impediments, and its social counterfeits.

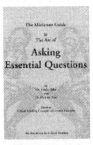

The Art of Asking Essential Questions—Focuses on the realization that the quality of your life is determined by the quality of your questions. Introduces critical thinking concepts and tools that enable you to ask questions that are more clear, precise, significant, and deep.

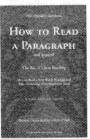

How to Read a Paragraph: The Art of Close Reading—Begins with the premise that to read closely is to engage in a disciplined process that enables you to construct accurately the meaning of the texts you read, to construct the thinking of an author in your own mind. This guide provides theory and activities necessary to develop your ability to read closely.

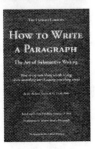

How to Write a Paragraph: The Art of Substantive Writing—Begins with the premise that to write substantively is to say something worth saying about something worth saying something about. It involves the ability to identify important ideas and express significant implications of them in clear and precise writing. This guide provides theory and activities for developing the art of substantive writing.

Notes

Notes

Notes

Notes

Notes

FutureThink
How to Think Clearly in a Time of Change
BY EDIE WEINER AND ARNOLD BROWN

16 Proven Mental Paths to Insight and Foresight

Being right about the future is critical...but it's not enough. You ne
to believe what you see and respond to it. That requires a fundam
tally new and better way of thinking. In *FutureThink*, Edie Weiner a
Arnold Brown share the techniques they've used to help hundre
of leading enterprises—including 3M, Merck, and the IRS—anticip
the future and act quickly on what they've learned, to get a powe
jumpstart on the competition.

- **Revealing the hidden patterns of change**
  Trend/countertrend, spirals and pendulums, extremes and middl
  multiplier effects, and more
- **The Law of Large Numbers: Explaining many of today's mo:
  powerful forces**
  Recognizing the drivers behind everything from deviancy to
  terrorism
- **Beyond "inattentional" blindness: Seeing what's coming up
  behind you**
  Practical techniques for supercharging your peripheral vision

ISBN 013185674X, © 2006, 304 pp., $24.99

The Right Decision Every Time
How to Reach Perfect Clarity on Tough Decisions
BY LUDA KOPEIKINA

**Breakthrough, MIT-developed techniques for making faster,
better decisions!**

Gain unprecedented clarity in all your decision-making so that you
can make consistently better decisions—and make them more rap-
idly. Drawing on her breakthrough research with 115 CEOs, Luda Kopeikina offers practical, proven techniques for structuring decisions,
achieving clarity about the real issues involved, and using that clarity
to improve the quality of every decision you make. Kopeikina begins
by defining clarity in decision-making, identifying five root causes for
decision difficulty, and introducing the "Clarity State": that singular
moment of focus where insights are triggered, things fall into place,
and solutions become obvious. Next, she introduces a set of powerful
techniques for overcoming decision difficulties, stripping away decision complexity. Kopeikina concludes with a case study tracing how
a real executive used these techniques to make a crucial strategic
decision. The book contains a convenient insert summarizing these
techniques for easy use "on the road." Using Kopeikina's approach, a
stunning 93% of CEOs made clear strategic decisions within 90 minutes or less—even when these decisions had been sitting unresolved
for weeks or months. You can be every bit as effective.

ISBN 0131862626, © 2006, 288 pp., $27.99